Baptist Mission Portraits

Smyth & Helwys Publishing, Inc.®
Macon, Georgia

Baptist Mission Portraits

by
John Allen Moore

Smyth & Helwys Publishing, Inc.®
Macon, Georgia

ISBN 1-880837-79-X

Baptist Mission Portraits
by John Allen Moore

Copyright © 1994
Smyth & Helwys Publishing, Inc.®

The paper used in this publication meets the minimum
requirements of American Standard for Information Sciences—
Permanence of paper for Printed Library Materials,
ANSI Z39.48-1984.

Library of Congress Cataloging-in-Publication Data

Moore, John Allen
    Baptist mission portraits/John Allen Moore
    viii + 171pp.   (6" x 9") (15 X 23 cm.)
    ISBN 1-880837-79-X
    1. Baptists—Missions—History. 2. Missionaries—Biography
I. Title.
BV2520.M75   1994
266'.61'0922—dc20   93-48140
[B]   CIP

Contents

To my wonderful wife,
Pauline Willingham Moore,
niece of our denomination's foreign mission director 1893–1917,
a missionary in Europe for four decades,
and an enterprising activist,
even in retirement and advanced age,
in mission education, promotion, and support.

Foreword

Someone has said that a great life is a banquet to which all are invited. In his own way each of the lives presented in this volume is great—as a pioneer in some aspect of Christian mission, in strength of character, and in steadfastness to the end.

As to length, it is a great advantage to a writer to have the liberty of allowing the story of a life to take its natural course until the writer's purpose is achieved. I have exercised this liberty, and the result is some short pieces and some pieces much longer. My intention is to give a fair and balanced portrait of each subject, not a panegyric nor the opposite. Each chapter is intended to be complete in itself, which necessarily involves incidental repetition in a few places.

Recently published books have furnished helpful insights or information, but many quotations come ultimately from letters, personal journals, and documents. The remainder come from very old publications.

Many thanks to readers for meeting—or getting better acquainted with—six of my friends from the past.

I wish to express appreciation to those persons in the U.S., England, India, and Burma (now Myanmar) who—on my visits in these lands—made available information about the life and work of the subjects in this collection. In past years I have written articles about these characters for publication in European countries and the U.S. Special thanks are due Leland Webb and the staff of *The Commission* (periodical of the Foreign Mission Board, SBC, Richmond, Virginia), who were cooperative and helpful.

John Allen Moore

William Carey—
He Could Persevere

Often called "the father of modern missions," William Carey surely deserves the title more than anyone else. He was not the first missionary to go to a foreign land, even in the rather dreary and formal eighteenth century. A considerable number of Roman Catholics, Moravians, and a few others had gone out and served sacrificially. Carey made a unique contribution, however.

He pioneered in the development of missionary principles as well as in the working out of these principles on the field and through supporters in the homeland. His insistent advocacy brought about the formation of a voluntary society, the first of its kind, for the purpose of sending missionaries to unevangelized peoples of the world. The society did not limit itself to work in the homeland and the British colonies, as earlier groups in England and Scotland had.

Perhaps Carey's chief contribution was in his sterling example of personal commitment, persistence, simple and earnest faith, rock-ribbed integrity, hard work, loyalty to faithful colleagues and first of all to Christ.

Young Carey Finds His Way

Nothing in his background suggested future greatness. He was born in a poor weaver's cottage in Paulerspury, England, 17 August 1761. When he was six years old, the family moved to the village schoolhouse. The elder Carey had been appointed schoolmaster and clerk in the parish church. Will Carey sat under his father's teaching for six years, the only formal schooling he ever received.

Young Carey soon began to show a remarkable capacity for self-education, and this would characterize his entire life. As a boy he was a keen observer of plants, insects, and birds. He kept a collection of such things in his room. Will's uncle Peter had spent years as a British soldier in faraway Canada and was a gardener in Paulerspury. He gave his nephew much help in practical botany and gardening. Doubtless, Uncle Peter planted in the boy's mind some thoughts about people and cultures overseas.

Courage and persistence became evident in the early years. Will determined to climb the highest and most difficult trees. In attempting to reach a bird's nest near the top of a tree, he fell and sustained considerable injury. As soon as he was able to do so, he slipped out of the house to try the tree again. This time he succeeded. Reproached for taking the risk, Will said that if he started something he felt he just had to keep on until it was done.

He wanted to be a gardener and tried this work for about two years. Due to some skin ailment, exposure to the sun brought unbearable irritation to face and hands. The elder Carey then apprenticed him to Clarke Nichols, a shoemaker in Piddington, eight or nine miles away.

Nichols, a staunch Church of England man, was seemingly a hard master, rough in language and a rather heavy drinker. None of this bothered Will much, but he later spoke with remorse of his own conduct and profanity of this period. One incident he related afterward "with a mixture of horror and gratitude."

It was a custom in that part of the country that apprentices be allowed during the Christmas season to collect for themselves small gratuities from the tradesmen with whom their masters had dealings. William, on an errand to an ironmonger in a nearby community, was given a shilling that he put immediately into his pocket. Next, he wanted to purchase some small items for himself. He then discovered that the shilling was a brass counterfeit.

He paid for his little purchase with a shilling of his master's, determined to insist strenuously that the bad money was his. William promised God that if he would get him safely through the deception, he would in the future leave off all evil practices.

As Carey later recounted this experience, he said that God, by God's grace, did not get him safely through it. Clarke Nichols sent his other apprentice to investigate, and the ironmonger confessed to giving William a counterfeit shilling. Young Carey was so overwhelmed with shame that he would not go out until he was assured the story of his dishonesty had not been spread over town.

Nichols's senior apprentice was John Warr, several of whose family members belonged to a small dissenting congregation nearby. (Dissenters rejected membership in the Church of England, the Anglican state church.) The two young men had many discussions on religion. Reared in an Anglican family that took the established religion and morals seriously, William was brought face to face for the first time with the question of personal and experiential faith.

He began attending dissenters' meetings, sometimes with John Warr. One of these gatherings was in the adjacent village of Hackleton on a Wednesday in February 1779. The king had proclaimed it a day of prayer in connection with reverses being suffered by British troops while trying to put down the rebellion of American colonists.

The preacher that day spoke on Hebrews 13:13: "Let us go forth therefore unto him without the camp, bearing his reproach." Carey made what he later called "very crude" application of these words—that the established church was "the camp in which all were protected from the scandal of the cross, and that I ought to bear the reproach of Christ among the dissenters." Carey joined the Hackleton group.

Clarke Nichols died suddenly and young Carey transferred to master shoemaker Thomas Old of Hackleton, who, along with other members of his family, held membership in the dissident congregation there.

In June 1781, William Carey married Dorothy Plackett, sister of Mrs. Old. He was not quite twenty; his bride was more than five years older. She, being illiterate, signed the marriage registry with a cross. Although very different in qualities of mind and will, they seemed to be a happy couple.

From the age of twelve Carey had studied languages and other subjects on his own. He borrowed books and secured a little help from those who had some classical education. He taught himself Latin and Greek and later Hebrew, Dutch, French, and a smattering of Italian.

On Sundays when he had no preaching appointment, he tramped many miles to hear not only dissenting but state-church preachers. His favorite was Thomas Scott, evangelical-minded Anglican minister in Olney. Afterward Carey wrote: "If there be any thing of the work of God in my soul, I owe much of it to Mr. Scott's preaching, when I first set out in the ways of the Lord."

Scott, in turn, was greatly impressed with Carey's wide-ranging interests, his keeping a book before him as he worked, and his well-ordered thinking about important subjects. William Carey, he said, would prove to be "no ordinary character." Long afterward, Scott remarked to a friend as they walked past what had been shoemaker Old's house and workshop, "That was Mr. Carey's college."

Further guidance for the scholarly young cobbler came from a book that a ministerial friend gave to him: *Help to Zion's Travelers* was a small volume by Robert Hall Sr., Baptist minister in the village of Arnsby. It sought to "remove various stumbling blocks in the way of doctrinal, experimental (sic), and practical religion." It appealed to thoughtful Christians and opposed prevalent hyper-Calvinism's rigid doctrine of election, insisting on the ability and duty of everyone to receive the gospel of Christ. Carey penned in his neat handwriting careful summaries on each page. Later he wrote, "I do not remember ever to have read any book with such raptures."

A daughter, Ann, was born to the Careys in 1781. The following year she and her father became ill with high fever, from which Ann died. William suffered for eighteen months with ague—bouts of chills, fever, and cough—that left him bald at the age of twenty-two. For the rest of his time in England he wore a cheap, ill-fitting wig.

Lay Preacher and Village Pastor

Thomas Old died, as suddenly as had Clarke Nichols, and the young journeyman shoemaker carried on the shoemaking business alone. He managed somehow to pay Mrs. Old for the time remaining on his period of training, although there was no obligation to do this. He had to work even harder—especially in the buying, repairing, and selling of used shoes. To find customers, he had to walk, with bags of shoes on his back, to many villages of the area.

Carey returned to Piddington where he opened a small school to supplement his meager income from shoe work. He remained a member of the Hackleton dissenting congregation. In 1882 a similar group in Earls Barton, six miles away, engaged him as lay preacher. For three and one-half years he walked there and back two Sundays a month for this largely unremunerated service. One Sunday a month he ministered to such a group in his native Paulerspury. He asked permission and was allowed to conduct family worship from time to time in his parents' home. There his two sisters were won to personal faith.

Carey undertook serious study of the Bible in Hebrew and Greek. He was convinced that baptism was for believers only. On his request he was baptized at the age of twenty-two in the River Nen by the young Baptist pastor John Ryland of Northampton, but he retained membership with the dissenters of Hackleton.

John Sutcliff, Baptist pastor in Olney, suggested he "join some church more respectable than that of Hackleton and be regularly sent into the ministry." Carey saw the wisdom of this and joined the Olney Baptist congregation. He preached for the people there and after many delays by the church was ordained in August 1786.

Meanwhile, he had moved to the village of Moulton, about five miles north of Earls Barton. There he opened a school and pursued his shoemaking trade. Moulton had a Baptist church, but it was small and weak, having been pastorless for the past ten years. Its meeting house, practically unused for a long time, was in a sad state of disrepair.

Members took heart at the coming of Carey to their community and called him as their pastor. They were able to pay only about ten pounds a year (then about forty-five dollars). This was supplemented by about half as much more from a pastoral aid fund in London. The new pastor had to continue his shoemaking and teaching to make ends meet. Even so, funds were so low he was unable to buy food to provide adequate diet for his family.

Carey enlivened classes in his little school, especially geography, by pasting sheets together to make a large map. On this he marked out each area of the world and wrote pertinent information. After seeing an advertisement in the *Northampton Mercury* offering "globes for use in schools" and being unable to buy one, he made his own globe of leather, with countries marked in varied coloring.

The Careys lived in Moulton four and one-half years. During this time William's beloved mother died, three sons were born to William and Dorothy, and William had the joy of baptizing Dorothy. Also, the idea of world mission began to possess Carey's mind. "My attention to missions was first awakened after I was in Moulton," Carey said later, "by reading the *Last Voyage of Captain Cook*." Cook's journals gave information about eastern lands, Pacific islands, and other areas previously unknown to the people of Britain.

As Carey studied and taught, he saw not just quaint and interesting tribes but numerous peoples in the thralldom of heathenism with no knowledge of the liberating gospel. He filled in as he was able the information on his wall map for each area as to size, population, and religion.

Not long after his ordination he attended a gathering of ministers following an associational meeting in Northampton. Elderly John Collett Ryland, father of the minister who had baptized Carey, invited the younger men to suggest subjects for discussion. After a pause, Carey in a humble manner proposed that they consider "whether the command given to the apostles to teach all nations was not obligatory on all succeeding ministers to the end of the world, seeing that the accompanying promise was of equal extent."

Ryland was a strong Calvinist, emphasizing God's predetermined election of those chosen for salvation, and he had a reputation for bombastic expression. He was reported to have snapped, "Young man, sit down. When God pleases to convert the heathen he will do it without your aid or mine!" Although there is some disagreement as to what Ryland actually said, obviously he denounced Carey with a sharp retort against human effort in missions until there should be a new Pentecost with a renewal of miraculous gifts as with the apostles in the beginning.

The Baptist cause prospered in Moulton under Carey's leadership. The meeting house had to be enlarged. Once when the pastor was in Birmingham collecting money for rebuilding the chapel, Carey was questioned about his missionary ideas by a well-to-do Baptist layman. On his initiative this man gave ten pounds for publishing the book on missions that Carey was preparing.

Andrew Fuller, Baptist pastor in Kettering, visited Moulton and learned of Carey's extensive studies and other work. He discussed this with one of his deacons, a merchant who bought most of the shoes Carey made. Informed that Carey earned nine or ten shillings a week with his shoemaking, the merchant told him to continue his study of Latin, Hebrew, and Greek and promised to provide Carey—from his private funds—ten shillings a week. This he apparently did, and Carey had more time for his studies.

In 1789 Carey received a probationary call from Harvey Lane Chapel in the town of Leicester and moved there with his family. Twenty-two months later he was formally installed as pastor. Churches of the time seem to have moved slowly in their decisions and actions.

Harvey Lane Chapel was in a morally deplorable condition when Carey arrived. Deacons and other members had been excluded for drunkenness. He led in the radical move of dissolving the church and beginning anew with only those who would engage in a solemn promise to try to live by New Testament standards. The pastor remained three and a half years with Harvey Lane, and the church doubled in membership. A balcony had to be added in the meeting house.

Carey's self-education continued. He wrote to his father, who was a sympathetic counselor: "On Monday I confine myself to the study of science, history, composition, etc. On Wednesday I preach a lecture. . . . On Thursday I visit my friends. Friday and Saturday are spent in preparing for the Lord's day." He mentioned regular preaching appointments not only at Harvey Lane but in two or three villages.

"My school," William went on in the letter to his father, "begins at nine o'clock in the morning and continues till four o'clock in winter and five in summer." Harvey Lane paid somewhat more than Moulton, but—despite every economy—the minister found it necessary to keep a school and practice his trade of shoemaking.

A daughter, Lucy, was born to the Careys in Leicester, but she died the following year.

Birth of the Unique Society

Carey pressed among his fellow ministers the matter of a mission to the "heathen." Fuller, Sutcliff, Samuel Pearce of Birmingham, and a few others were interested, but it seemed to them too great an undertaking for small Baptist churches in the Midlands of England. They suggested, perhaps to gain time in the face of Carey's persistence, that he publish the book he had prepared about missions, and he did.

The eighty-seven page book is entitled, *An Enquiry into the Obligations of Christians to Use Means for the Conversion of the Heathens.* After an introduction, Carey began with the Great Commission and considered objections to mission work.

> Many say that the commission was sufficiently put into execution by what the apostles and others have done; that we have enough to do to attend to the salvation of our own countrymen; and that, if God intends the salvation of the heathen he will some way or other bring them to the gospel, or the gospel to them. These critics of mission work maintain that the apostles were a special group with no proper successors, and what was assigned to them is not binding on ministers later.

Carey wrote long afterward to Fuller that this section was his considered reply to the elderly Ryland's denunciation of Carey's suggestion of the subject at the ministers' meeting in 1785.

The author gave a survey of missionary activities as recorded in the book of Acts, then cited some examples in the succeeding centuries and the Middle Ages. For the two centuries previous to his writing, Carey could point to only a few sporadic efforts among the Indians of America and some other groups in various parts of the world. He commended especially the Moravians and pointed out their widespread fields of labor.

A large section of the book was given to a statistical survey. The author estimated the world population of the time at about 731,000,000. Approximately one-fourth of the people bore the Christian name—Catholics, Eastern Orthodox, Protestants, and others. The author listed size, estimated population, and religion for each area of the world.

Carey offered practical suggestions about home supporters, qualifications of missionaries, learning of foreign languages, and ways in which missionaries could largely support themselves in the manner of the Moravians.

The author appealed to all denominations but recognized that any early and effective action would come from his own little group of associates. He said:

> In the present divided state of Christendom, it would be more likely for good to be done by each denomination engaging separately in the work. . . . There is room enough for us all.

Carey was invited to preach at the next associational meeting, to be held in Nottingham at the end of May 1792. He took as his text Isaiah 54:2-3: "Enlarge the place of thy tent . . . lengthen thy cords and strengthen thy stakes . . . and thy seed shall inherit the Gentiles." He fervently appealed, under two points, for bold mission effort: (1) expect great things; (2) attempt great things. Later accounts added "from God" to the first point and "for God" to the second. Carey made clear in his sermon that any success in missions would come from God, to whose purposes the entire effort must be directed.

The following morning the ministers met for the transaction of associational business. The issue that Carey had urged came up for discussion. Most of the ministers were quite poor and felt keenly their lack of influence in the denomination. Most favored delay. In his distress near the end of the meeting, Carey seized Fuller's arm and exclaimed, "Is nothing, again, going to be done?" Galvanized into action by his friend's plea, Fuller made a motion—which was accepted—"that a plan be prepared against the next ministers' meeting at Kettering for forming a Baptist Society for propagating the Gospel among the heathens."

The fall meeting of the association took place at Fuller's church in Kettering on 2 October 1792. Ryland and Pearce preached. In the evening, fourteen of the participants—twelve pastors, a ministerial student, and a deacon—were guests in the home of widow Beeby Wallis. After the meal, they withdrew to the twelve-feet-by-ten feet back parlor for their ministerial discussions.

When other business had been attended to they took up the matter of the mission "plan." Many still wavered, stymied by the magnitude of the idea. They were inclined for the most part to drop it, for the time being at least. Desperate, Carey pulled from his pocket the latest issue of the *Periodical Accounts of Moravian Missions*. If the others could just read this material, he said, they would see how obstacles might be overcome and the work go forward in faith. He related mission victories that were reported in the periodical. This challenging presentation seemed somehow to win the day. Fuller, Pearce, Sutcliff, and the younger Ryland strongly supported Carey. The entire group agreed on this founding statement:

> Desirous of making an effort for the propagation of the Gospel among the heathen, agreeably to what is recommended in brother Carey's late publication on that subject, we, whose names appear to the subsequent subscription, do solemnly agree to act in society together for that purpose. . . . It is agreed that this society be called *The Particular Baptist Society for Propagating the Gospel among the Heathen*.

Fuller's emptied snuff box was passed around to collect slips of paper on which participants wrote their pledges. John Ryland promised two guineas (a guinea was a shilling over a pound), Reynold Hogg the same amount. Six men pledged a guinea, and five men pledged half a guinea each. Altogether thirteen pounds, two and one-half shillings—perhaps about $58.30 in U.S. money at the time—were pledged to begin Baptist world mission work. Anyone giving at least ten shillings and sixpence (half a guinea) a year would be counted a member of the society. Carey did not pledge but gave instead all income from sales—past, present, and future—of his *Enquiry*.

The ministerial student, not yet a pastor, who took part in this meeting signed himself simply "Anon. 10/6." He was in fact William Staughton, who would become an eloquent preacher, a college president, and staunch mission leader in the United States.

Ryland, Hogg, Carey, Sutcliff, and Fuller were named as an executive committee of the society, which Fuller would serve as general secretary. Sutcliff, at age forty, was oldest of the leaders.

Pledge of the Rope-Holders

Months later Carey received a letter from a doctor, John Thomas, who resided in London. Thomas wrote that he had intended to be at the Kettering meeting but forgot the date. It was typical of this greathearted blunderer, who would bring much sorrow to the mission, though he served it very well indeed on several important occasions. Thomas had been a ship's surgeon, then he settled in the province of Bengal in India at two different periods for a total of five or six years. He learned the Bengali language. An earnest Christian and a licensed Baptist minister, he had preached to the Bengalis and served them well with his medical skill.

Knowing of this man only what Thomas himself had written, Carey wrote the mission committee that Thomas was

> trying to establish a fund in London for a mission to Bengal; he ardently desires a companion. . . . Would it not be worthy of the society to try to make that and ours unite into one fund for the purpose of sending the gospel to the heathen?

Fuller made inquiries in London about Thomas, then met the man and arranged for him to attend the next meeting of the committee on 9 January, 1793. Thomas assured Fuller and the others that a missionary in Bengal could build a good house with mud walls and straw roof for about seventeen shillings. Chickens were available for a penny each, he said, a lamb for eightpence, and so on. As in everything regarding business, Thomas was wrong in these estimates.

He later notified the committee that due to a foot injury he would not be able to attend the meeting on 9 January. On the evening of that day, however, as the group was concluding its long periods of discussion, Thomas hobbled in. Members reassembled to hear a report from him. He gave glowing descriptions of the opportunity in India. He confessed to serious personal financial obligations but hoped to solve the problem.

The committee asked Thomas if he would go to India as its missionary, and he readily agreed, requesting at the same time an associate. Carey offered to go with him, and they were appointed "to the East Indies for preaching the gospel to the heathen."

How would Carey break the news to his wife, who had the care of three children and was expecting another? She had never traveled more than forty miles from her birthplace. When William told her of the plan for a mission in faraway India, she refused to go. Carey's father, when he heard of the plan, exclaimed, "Is William mad?"

Fuller and Sutcliff tried to persuade Dorothy Carey but to no avail. It was finally decided that her husband would proceed with the oldest son Felix, who was eight, then return in perhaps three years or so for the remainder of the family. Carey arranged to settle his wife and the younger children in her native village, Piddington.

The society had raised about 130 pounds in all, but the estimated cost of passage for the two Careys, Thomas, his wife and little daughter would be at least 150 pounds. The society needed also to send supplies for sale in India to support the missionaries for a year until they could be settled and largely self-supporting.

On Carey's last Sunday as pastor, according to his biographer S. Pearce Carey, a businessman from Yorkshire visited the services. He described in a letter the obvious grief of the people at the realization they were losing their beloved pastor. This visitor asked Carey, following the afternoon service, whether he felt peace of mind in what he was doing. Carey replied in the affirmative, declaring that his family and friends were dear to him, and that he was saddened at the thought of leaving them, but he felt God's clear call to the mission and was happy in obeying that call.

The farewell service came three days later on 20 March in the Leicester church with Thomas and Hogg preaching. Fuller delivered the farewell address on goals of the mission, instructions for the missionaries, difficulties to be anticipated, and rewards expected. The mission committee promised to take care of Carey's family.

Sometime late that evening the men of the inner circle—Fuller, Ryland, Sutcliff, Pearce, and Carey—managed to meet together for the last time. They talked of the task ahead. Carey drew the group into a covenant that pledged—as he and Thomas went out in the name of the society and of Christ—these men"should never cease till death to stand by him." Fuller later described it:

Our understanding in India really appeared at its beginning to me some-what like a few men, who were deliberating about the importance of penetrating a deep mine, which had never before been explored. We had no one to guide us; and, whilst we were thus deliberating, Carey, as it were, said, "Well, I will go down, if you will hold the rope." But before he descended, he, as it seemed to me, took an oath from each of us at the mouth of the pit, to this effect, that "whilst we lived, we should never let go of the rope."

Carey, Thomas, and Fuller itinerated among the churches to raise funds for the mission.

Getting to India

The East India Company, formed in 1600, had a monopoly on British trade in India and exercised practically all of British authority there. Only the company's ships sailed from Britain for India ports. The company was hostile to anything like missionary work, contending that disturbance of religious beliefs and customs would make for disorder and rebellion. Theoretically, for anyone to visit or reside in British India without a license from the company was a high crime, punishable with fines and imprisonment. No licenses were available for missionaries.

Thomas had served as surgeon on the *Earl of Oxford* and knew its captain, who agreed to assume the risk of taking Carey and Thomas to India without a permit. Arrangements were made. Carey, his son Felix, and Thomas and his wife and daughter went on board, along with all the baggage—including the goods for sale in India. The vessel sailed on schedule from its docks on the Thames River. The revolution in France and resulting wars were in progress, however, and the English Channel swarmed with French privateers. The *Earl of Oxford* had to put in at the Isle of Wight to wait for a convoy. The missionary party took lodgings on shore.

One day a business agent arrived there, accompanied by a bailiff and demanding to see Thomas, who was away in London. Carey learned to his consternation that the visitor represented some of Thomas's creditors who were demanding payment. The poor man's pressing debts totaled about five hundred pounds. He had previously bought goods in India that had to be sold in England at far below cost.

While at the Isle of Wight, Carey received a letter from his wife informing him of the birth of a son whom she named Jabez (sorrowful). She asked what William's state of mind was by this time, in connection with his undertaking and departure. He replied:

> It is much as when I left you. If I had all the world, I would freely give it all to have you and my dear children with me; but the sense of duty is so strong as to overpower all other considerations; I could not turn back without guilt on my soul. . . . Trust in God. . . . Be assured I love you most affectionately.

Someone at the company's India House in London wrote the ship's captain, warning that one of his passengers had no permit and threatening that if this person were taken anyway the captain would lose his command. This risk was too great for him, and he was ready to sail. The captain had the baggage belonging to Carey and Thomas taken off the ship and stored on shore. He had no objection to Mrs. Thomas. She and her daughter remained on board and sailed away to India.

In the first of Thomas's flashes of helpful service to the mission, he found out by devious inquiries in a London coffee house that a non-British ship would sail for India. A waiter furtively slipped into his hand a small piece of paper on which was written: "A Danish East India man, No. 10 Cannon St." At this address Thomas and Carey found "Smith and Co., Agents" and learned that Smith's brother captained a Danish ship that was sailing from Copenhagen to Calcutta. It would not dock but just halt off Dover, probably not more than five days later. There were several unoccupied berths, and prices were one hundred pounds for adults, fifty pounds for children, and twenty-five pounds for attendants or servants.

The would-be voyagers had only 150 pounds sterling returned by the captain of the *Earl of Oxford*. Thomas suggested that Carey and his son use this money and go—he would follow at the next opportunity. Carey loyally declined. He did desire to use these days, however, to return and see whether his wife had perhaps changed her mind about accompanying him. Her pregnancy had been one of the reasons she gave for not going. The two men hoped also to raise further funds.

Carey and Thomas rode the stagecoach all night to Northampton, then walked to Piddington early on a Saturday morning. Carey's wife remained adamant in the decision not to go to India. Sadly, the two men departed. They trudged unhappily down the Northampton highroad for about half a mile. Suddenly Thomas stopped. "I will go back," he said.

"Well, do as you think proper," Carey murmured, "but I think we are losing time." He made no move and Thomas started off alone. After a few moments, however, Carey followed. When they reached the cottage, Thomas warned Mrs. Carey that her decision meant "the family would be dispersed and divided, perhaps for ever," and that "she would repent of it as long as she lived." This heartbreaking thought demolished her resistance. She said she would go if her sister Katherine, who was listening to the conversation, would accompany her. The brave sister, after prayer about it, agreed to do so.

This came as a happy turn of events for Carey and Thomas, but it magnified their financial problem. It added two adults and Carey's other three boys to the party. The two men rushed off to Northampton, while the women tried to prepare within a few hours for departure to the other side of the world.

Dr. Ryland in Northampton gave letters for friends in London to advance two hundred pounds in the name of the mission. The total needed now, however, totaled about seven hundred pounds, double the amount available.

Generous, warm-hearted Thomas came to the rescue again. He worked out a scheme whereby he and Katherine Plackett would travel as attendants, living and eating with servants on the ship, while the Careys would have regular accommodations. Thomas offered Smith and Company three hundred pounds for the entire group, and these very modest terms were accepted.

The Carey family and Katherine Plackett proceeded to Dover to await the ship, *Kron Princessa Maria*. Thomas had to get the baggage from Portsmouth by sea. Haggling for two days with boatmen about the cost of this dangerous service—because of the French privateers—he was terrified lest he get to Dover too late.

The ship was delayed by contrary winds, however, and did not pick up the mission party until 13 June.

The ship's captain, English born and bred, had become a naturalized Dane and called himself Captain Christmas. He refused to place Thomas and Katherine Plackett with the servants but provided them good quarters and meals with the Careys at his own table.

The voyage took five months and ended 11 November 1793. For the last month the party was within about two hundred miles of the Bengal coast, held back by contrary winds and strong currents. Thomas gave Carey lessons in Bengali during the voyage. They began Bible translation and completed in some fashion the book of Genesis. Carey was planning for the future. He wrote in his journal:

> I am very desirous that my children may pursue the same works and now intend to bring up one in the study of Sanscrit, and another of Persian. O May God give them grace to fit them for the work!

Attempting to Settle Down

Before reaching Calcutta, which was farther up the Hoogli River, the mission party transferred to a smaller boat. Soon this little craft had to put in to a landing place to await the ebbing tide. Carey and Thomas disembarked, and Thomas preached three hours in Bengali at the marketplace of a nearby village. Someone provided rice, curry, and fruits to the visitors. They sat on the ground and ate in the Indian way, using plantain leaves as plates and taking the food up with their fingers. Carey was most impressed by the teeming masses of people, suggesting great possibilities for evangelism. This was said to be the most densely populated area of the world at the time.

The next day the Carey family, Katherine, and Thomas slipped off the boat at Calcutta, arranging for their baggage also, "without being molested or even noticed." Calcutta then had a population of about 200,000—Bengal as a whole claiming 25,000,000. Thomas found his wife and daughter, then looked up a few persons he had on previous visits regarded as converts or inquirers. One of these, Ram Ram Basu, became language teacher and pundit for Carey.

Thomas sold the stock of goods brought for support of the mission families the first year, but this yielded much less than the 150 pounds expected. He spent the money freely without consulting his fellow missionary, and it diminished rapidly. Carey was able for a time to house his family rent-free in the garden house of an Indian gentleman, while Thomas set up practice as a physician in Calcutta.

"I am in a strange land alone," Carey wrote in his personal journal, "no Christian friends, a large family, and nothing to supply their wants." Even on the darkest days, however, there was never the least suggestion of a thought to give up on the mission.

Carey managed to secure from the authorities, rent-free for three years, a tract of land in the Sunderbuns, a tiger-infested jungle area of the Ganges delta southeast of Calcutta. When he went to Thomas to obtain funds for traveling to the place, he learned that their mission money was gone—three weeks from the time of arrival. The doctor was living in relative luxury with many servants, and he had borrowed more money! Carey himself was obliged to borrow at a high rate of interest to cover expenses for his family's three-day boat trip to settle in the Sunderbuns early in 1794.

When Carey's family members arrived at their destination, the village of Deharta, the first person they met was an Englishman, Charles Short. He represented the East India Company's salt department for the district. Short considered himself a deist and was not at all interested in mission work. He heartily welcomed the Carey party, however, and urged them to live in his spacious home, even for a year if needful. Carey thankfully accepted, although he was inwardly embarrassed to receive such generosity from one so unsympathetic with his purpose for being in India. Carey planned to clear the land and build a house for his large family as soon as possible, then plant crops for their support.

He had many talks with Short about spiritual matters and eventually led him to personal faith in Christ. Charles Short married Katherine Plackett, and somewhat later they returned to England, where he remained a loyal supporter of the British mission.

Carey's wife suffered for many months with dysentery, often with high fever, as did two of the sons. Discomforts and uncertainties of this period intensified physical and emotional problems for Dorothy Carey. She criticized and complained. Sometimes her sister joined in. Dorothy could not be of much help in caring for the family. Carey wrote in his journal:

> My wife, and sister too, who do not see the importance of the mission as I do, are continually exclaiming against me. . . . If my family were but hearty in the work, I should find a great burden removed.

Carey realized that his wife suffered also from mental illness.

Despite all the difficulties, Carey felt optimistic about the work and planned to serve indefinitely where he was. The soil was rich. The varied flora and fauna intrigued him as a careful student of natural history. The people, he hoped, would be open to the gospel. With the help of his pundit, he continued his study of the Bengali language. His journal is replete with self reproach for not being more spiritual, but he remained firm in his faith that God would accomplish his purpose in India.

The Careys had been in the Sunderbuns a few weeks and the construction of their bamboo house was far advanced when the course of events began to change again. On the first day of March Carey received a letter from Thomas, who apologized for his conduct in Calcutta. He told of being in contact again with George Udney, the company's commercial resident in Malda. Udney had helped support Thomas when he was earlier in India then broke with him because of his irresponsible ways.

Udney was opening two new indigo "factories" where juice was extracted from the plant and processed into cakes of blue dye. He offered Thomas the post as manager of one of the factories. Thomas accepted and asked if Carey could have the other. Udney agreed. Each manager would receive a salary of two hundred rupees a month (about $120 in U.S. money at that time), with promise of part ownership later.

Thomas chose the plant at Moypaldiggy, which left Mudnabatty (seventeen miles away) for Carey. "Nothing yields me more pleasure," generous Carey wrote, "than the prospect of Mr. Thomas and I being reunited in the work." He referred of course to mission work, which Carey always kept in first place. Because of George Udney's position, there was no problem in getting five-year residence and work permits from East India Company officials for Thomas and Carey.

After nearly three months of making all arrangements for the move to Mudnabatty, on 23 May the Carey party started on the three-hundred-mile river journey of three weeks to Malda. The river was so crooked that for one section it took two days to make what would have been four miles in a straight line. The lack of roads made travel by water necessary. By this time Carey could speak some Bengali, and he proclaimed the Christian gospel to groups of interested people in villages along the way.

Carey wrote to Fuller, in view of the regular income anticipated, freeing the society from further financial responsibility for support of the Careys:

> At the same time, it will be my glory and joy to stand in the same near relation to the society as if I needed supplies from them, and to maintain the same correspondence with them.

He did request that they send certain books and simple farming tools, as well as seeds for vegetables, flowers, and fruit trees—the cost for which he would remit to the society from his earnings. This was all for the betterment, Carey wrote, of what he now called "my own country."

He did suggest that Thomas receive a regular allowance from the society so that he could apply it to his indebtedness. The poor man's creditors had been after him in India, and he had to borrow further in order to pay something on his debts so that he could stay out of jail.

No remittances had yet come from England, nor had anything else. Seventeen months after their arrival in India, the missionaries received the first parcel of letters, and later other remittances arrived. The total contributed by the society to support of the missionaries for the first three years was about two hundred pounds.

Indigo and Evangelism

Carey's letter telling of the new employment and freeing the society from his support was dealt with by the mission committee in Fuller's absence due to illness. The committee passed a resolution regarding Carey and Thomas that "a letter of serious and affectionate caution be addressed to them" about taking secular work, and this was done.

The insinuation—that they might become so involved in worldly business that they would neglect missionary work—hurt Carey deeply. In reference to the securing of employment for mission support, Carey replied:

> I always understood that the society recommended it. Trade in timber was recommended and cultivation of the ground. . . . We really thought we were acting in conformity with the universal wishes of the society. . . . After my family's obtaining a bare allowance, my whole income—and some months much more—goes for the purposes of the gospel . . . in supporting persons to assist in the translation of the Bible, write copies, teach school, and the like.

Carey's district of supervision in the cultivation of indigo was about twenty miles square and included approximately two hundred villages. Practically all the farmers grew indigo for the Mudnabatty plant. For travel, in his daily work, and in his gospel witness, Carey took one small boat for personal accommodations—bed, lamp, table, and chair—and another for the preparation of his meals. From where the boats were tied, he walked twelve to twenty miles a day to nearby villages. As always, he jotted down details of animal life, birds, insects, flowers, trees, and shrubs wherever he went.

In his indigo duties Carey supervised several hundred workers, which kept him quite busy three months of the year. Even in the busy period he did language study and translation and preached and witnessed personally to his faith regularly. In indigo's off-seasons he worked afternoons and evenings entirely in mission activities. He spent hours at a time in the market places speaking with people about the gospel and the futility of idol worship.

Carey held to a deep conviction that the immediate and essential task in winning India to Christ was translation of the Word of God into its languages. Discovering that the "dead" language Sanscrit was basic to most of India's languages, he undertook a serious study of it. At the same time, he was making good progress in translating the Bible into Bengali.

There were seemingly serious inquirers about the gospel, and Carey cherished high hopes that some of them would become Christians. None did, however, while he was in Mudnabatty. The people were quite willing to hear the preaching of the gospel, he said, but very slow in understanding and following it.

The prize convert of this period was a successful businessman of Portuguese descent, Ignatius Fernandez, who lived in Dinajpur, some distance north of Mudnabatty. The man had come years before from Macao to India as a priest's helper but had left Catholicism because of its veneration of images. Thomas seems to have been instrumental in his conversion.

Carey helped organize a Baptist church in Dinajpur, composed only of Europeans and Eurasians at that time. Thomas and Carey alternately made the trip there to preach. Fernandez later became pastor, giving generously of his time and money to varied mission activities. The missionaries named him "honorary missionary."

Fernandez continued his businesses, which included a candle factory. Carey had been using crude native lamps for his evening translation work and greatly appreciated the good supply of candles Fernandez sent to him regularly.

Carey was small of stature, bald, and somewhat stooped. His health remained generally good, but he had bouts with "fevers" that must have generally been malaria. His wife's mental condition worsened. She and the boys continued to suffer with dysentery, from which the third son, Peter, died at five years of age. Because of caste taboos and despite the fact that two carpenters were employed at his "factory," Carey could find no one who would make the coffin. It seemed that he, although ill at the time, would have to carry the small body to the grave. Finally, a boy from another village who had lost caste and was a cleaning servant agreed to bury the body.

William Carey, despite his courage and tenacity, was not a self-assured man. He described himself as "phlegmatic" and "cold," having "no love." "I am not one of those who are strong and do exploits," he wrote to a friend. "I often fear that instead of being instrumental in the conversion of the heathen, I may some time dishonor the cause in which I am engaged." On another occasion he wrote this note, "If God uses me, none need despair." He gave as his reason for never publishing anything of a specifically religious or devotional nature the fear that his life might later belie what he had written.

Still he was able to write to Samuel Pearce:

> I would not abandon the mission for all the fellowships and finest spheres in England. My greatest calamity would be separation from this service. . . . The work to which God has set his hands, will infallibly prosper.

This optimism as to the work of God prevailed over pessimism about his own character and service.

Carey continually begged the society for missionary recruits. They should be chosen carefully, he warned, full account being taken that the wives were "as hearty in the work as their husbands." This emphasis must have come out of Carey's hard experience.

A single new missionary, John Fountain, appeared on Carey's doorstep in 1796, without previous notice. He had been an ardent "republican," while England nervously feared revolution such as had occurred in France. He expressed some radical ideas even after arrival in India such as criticism of the all-powerful East India Company. His ideas upset Fuller, but Carey defended Fountain, who served the mission well in music and evangelism for the brief period of time left to him.

Thomas was, of course, unsuccessful at his indigo factory and left it after three years. He tried medical practice in Calcutta again, then moved his family to Nuddea where they lived in a boat. Afterward he rented an indigo plant, then superintended a sugar factory. In every such thing attempted, Thomas failed. Through it all, however, he strove earnestly to evangelize.

Carey saw a newspaper advertisement offering a wooden printing press for sale in Calcutta, and George Udney gave the forty pounds to buy it. The missionary had wanted a press to print tracts and the portions of the Bengali Bible that had been prepared. When the apparatus arrived in Mudnabatty and Carey explained to the curious villagers what it would do, they said to one another that it was the Englishman's idol.

Settling in Serampore

In the latter part of 1798 Carey was heartened by a letter from the mission committee stating that among new recruits would be the printer and editor, William Ward. The name brought back memories to the pioneer missionary. While he, Thomas, and Fuller were itinerating among churches to raise funds for the mission venture, he met the young man, who was then a printer in Derby. "If the Lord bless us," Carey said to him, "we shall want a person of your business to enable us to print the scriptures. I hope you will come after us." The idea stuck in young Ward's mind, and he took ministerial training to prepare himself.

George Udney suffered large losses in Calcutta investments, and floods ravaged his indigo crops year after year. He closed the indigo plants but paid Carey's salary several additional months to the end of 1799.

In order to save a base for the mission, Carey bought from Udney, mostly on credit, a small indigo plant in nearby Kidderpore. It was on somewhat higher ground than Mudnabatty. There he started building simple mission houses. He planned a self-supporting mission compound after the Moravian pattern whereby each family would have a little house to itself but would take meals with all the others to save money for the mission. Carey received word that the new missionaries were arriving and sent Fountain to Calcutta to meet them and bring them to Kidderpore.

William Ward appeared in Mudnabatty one Sunday morning, accompanied by John Fountain. Ward had come to Calcutta on an American ship along with the other new missionaries: Joshua and Hannah Marshman, the Grants, the Brunsdons, and Mary Tidd (who had come out to marry Fountain). Officials suspected them of spying for France and refused to issue permits for them to reside in British India. Even after authorities discovered their mistake they would not change the decision.

The missionaries brought with them from England a letter of introduction to Colonel Ole Bie, governor of the tiny Danish territory that the British called Serampore, and they proceeded to this place. There they planned to remain only until some arrangements could be made to move on to Kidderpore.

Governor Bie received the missionaries cordially and urged that they settle in Serampore, which was about fifteen miles upriver from Calcutta. The territory had about fifty houses at the time, and residents were of many different nationalities. The area around Serampore was thickly populated by Indians. Ward had been able to travel to Mudnabatty only because the friendly governor gave him a Danish passport. Ward and Fountain brought to Carey the proposal that the mission could move to Serampore.

Carey considered the matter very carefully. Mission work had started in the area where he worked and had bought property. Threats from influential persons in the district made it rather clear, however, that there might be little freedom for mission activities by a larger group. The new missionaries had no assurance that permits would ever be granted to them. Carey made the decision for Serampore and settled there with his family 10 January 1800. Fountain married Mary Tidd and they came to Serampore, also.

The new missionaries Grant and Brunsdon soon died, and John Fountain died in August 1800. Dysentery and other virulent diseases of the area were taking their toll.

Joshua and Hannah Marshman proved to be tremendous assets to the work, as did William Ward. They learned Bengali well. Men of the mission, including Fountain until his death, were active in almost-daily preaching and street evangelism in surrounding Indian villages. Opponents sometimes threw stones at them or made their evangelistic work difficult in other ways. Ward was thirty years of age, Marshman a year older, and Carey thirty-eight years-old as they began their work in and around Serampore.

They bought a large house near the riverbank for six thousand rupees, or 758 Pounds (c. $3,552)—as Carey reckoned value of the pound at the time. The rent for it would have reached this amount in about four years. Missionaries pooled their resources to make the down payment for the mission house. Later they were able to add some smaller buildings. For economical reasons, the entire group organized almost as one household. Each family or single unit had its own living quarters, but meals were taken together at four long tables. Domestic management devolved upon each missionary in turn for a month or more.

The group named Carey as permanent treasurer. All group members would join in making general decisions. On Carey's initiative in this, they differed from the Moravian mission plan. It called for a "house father, to whom the others should in love be subject." All income for members of the Serampore group would go into a common fund for mission work. From this each missionary would receive a small allowance for personal needs. When the plan was fully operational, Ward received twenty pounds a year, the Marshmans gained thirty-four pounds, and Carey with his larger family was given somewhat more.

The missionaries organized a Baptist church that met in the mission's chapel, and Carey served as pastor. Services were conducted in English and Bengali. Governor Bie and other Danes often attended the English services. The governor in effect turned over the pulpit of his Lutheran church in Serampore to the Baptist missionaries.

The Marshmans established schools, including one for girls, even though no Indian woman could read. Some of these schools proved to be lucrative, bringing in considerable profits, and others were free. Ward's printing, although mainly Bibles and tracts in various languages, produced some income also.

Thomas was not part of the Serampore group, but he did visit the missionaries there. In October of that first year he brought with him a Muslim sugar-boiler by the name of Fukeer, who seemed to be ready for full commitment to Christ. The little church assembly listened to his inspiring testimony then accepted him for baptism. He asked to make a visit to his village first. He departed and was not heard of again. Missionaries could not learn what had happened to him. Many suspected foul play by his family or Hindu associates.

The First Converts

About the time that Fukeer gave his testimony, about one-half mile from the Serampore mission house, a poor carpenter named Krishna Pal had a bad fall and dislocated his shoulder. In dreadful pain he sent for Thomas, who had previously spoken to him of Christ. The doctor rushed to Krishna's side, accompanied by Carey and Marshman. While these two held out Krishna's arm, Thomas jerked the bone back into its socket. In this moment of torture Krishna cried out for salvation from his sins. After the pain had eased somewhat, Thomas explained the gospel further to him, and Carey did the same when he came the next day to bring medicines.

As soon as he was able, Krishna began coming regularly to the mission for instruction, bringing with him his friend Gokul. Krishna soon reached full decision and requested baptism. He ate with the missionaries, thus breaking caste. He was baptized by Carey on 28 December 1800 in the Hoogly River at the Baptist mission's landing steps. Carey also baptized his own fifteen-year-old son, Felix, who had already been working with Ward in village evangelism. Krishna's wife and Gokul soon professed faith and joined the church, followed by several others. Krishna Pal became a faithful preacher and evangelist.

During the otherwise happy occasion of the baptism of the first Indian convert in over seven years of work by Carey and Thomas, the latter was confined in a room of the mission's school building "raving mad." Uncontrollable joy unhinged his reason. Carey's wife, chronically ill but now a danger to herself and others, was confined in another room. Missionaries had to place Thomas in a Calcutta insane asylum, but he was released after a month. He died in October 1801, in Fernandez' home in Dinajpur, where Fountain had died a year before.

Only three men were left in the mission, but they were giants: the "Serampore Trio"—Carey, Marshman, and Ward. Ward married Fountain's widow, and it was a happy union.

Despite the usual hostility of British authorities to missions, Governor-General Lord Wellesley came to appreciate Carey's proficiency in languages. Wellesley established Fort William College in

Calcutta for the training of British young men who came out to work in India's administration. Two Anglican chaplains who knew of Carey's linguistic and missionary work recommended him to the governor-general, who appointed him tutor of the Bengali language.

Carey felt reluctant to accept the position, feeling unqualified for it and fearing that it might interfere with his missionary service. His colleagues and the chaplains assured him that he was well able to do the teaching and that it would enhance the influence of his Bible translation and other mission activities.

Carey began teaching at Fort William College in May 1801. He did so well in Bengali that two other languages, including Sanscrit, were added to his responsibilities. Carey was ordinarily rowed in a small boat from the Serampore landing to Calcutta each Tuesday and back again Friday evening. Rarely he traveled in a horse-drawn buggy. After a few years he became full professor with a salary of fifteen hundred pounds a year, which went of course to the mission fund in Serampore.

Despite his many other mission activities, Bible translation remained Carey's chief pursuit. Even during the days he resided and taught in Calcutta, he kept several pundits busy. He reached a major milestone in March 1801 when a printed and bound copy of the Bengali New Testament, which had just appeared in an edition of two thousand copies, was placed on the communion table in the Serampore chapel. Experts said it was the first book ever published in Bengali for the general reader. It gave a literary character to the language.

Not long afterward, Carey completed the translation of the Old Testament in Bengali, and Ward printed the entire Bible. Carey added approximately one new language a year to his working knowledge. He worked closely with one or more pundits who were specialists in each language. With his helpers, he published the entire Bible in six languages of India and parts of it in about thirty more. Carey prepared grammars in six of the thirty languages and dictionaries in several of them. He translated some classical works for use in his college classes and otherwise.

At closing exercises of the third session of Fort William College, Carey's students made speeches before a large company including the governor-general, his brother (the future Duke of Wellington), and other British and Indian dignitaries. Carey addressed the gathering both in Bengali and in Sanscrit—the first speech ever delivered in that classical language by a European. Contrary to advice given to him, Carey declared openly in these speeches his primary work as a missionary and spoke of preaching daily to the Indian people. He commended Lord Wellesley for establishing the college and thus meeting a great need.

"I am much pleased with Mr. Carey's truly original and excellent speech," Wellesley declared. "I esteem such a testimony from such a man a greater honor than the applause of courts and parliaments." He said essentially the same thing in private to the missionary.

Another honor, the doctor of divinity degree, was awarded to Carey in 1807 by Brown University in Providence, Rhode Island.

Carey, supported by his missionary colleagues, asked British Baptists for forty missionaries to be sent immediately. This was not too great a number for 400 home churches to provide, he insisted.

The missionaries preached regularly in Calcutta, Serampore, and surrounding villages. They distributed tracts and Bible portions. Early in 1803 the first convert of the highest caste, a Brahmin, was baptized. He had come to serious consideration of the gospel by reading one of the mission tracts. By this time there were thirteen baptized Bengalis, several of them from the higher castes, and growth continued slowly but steadily after that.

Under Carey's lead, the mission determined that converts would not have their names changed to "Christian" names at baptism, and that in the Baptist churches no recognition should be given to caste. This decision created quite a sensation when a young Brahmin convert married the daughter of Krishna Pal.

Hampered by Government and by Fire

A new missionary joined the Baptist mission in 1803, and four others arrived two years later. Some of these succumbed to the Indian climate and diseases. Felix Carey helped start a mission in Burma, and the society in England recognized him as one of its missionaries. Two further recruits for the India mission, upon their arrival in 1806, received an order from authorities to return to England and meanwhile not to leave Calcutta.

There had been a mutiny of Indian soldiers in Vellore, a thousand miles away, seven weeks earlier. They massacred 114 officers and men. This was in no way connected with mission work. None existed in that part of India except for the labors of a few Catholics. Opponents of missions latched on to it anyway, saying that such violence resulted from the efforts of missionaries to introduce a new faith. Calcutta authorities nervously gave way to the agitation against mission work.

Carey, when he inquired of officials in Calcutta about the order against the new missionaries, was handed a notice for himself from the new governor-general, Sir George Barlow. It stated that, as the government did not interfere with the religious prejudices of the natives, neither should Mr. Carey and his colleagues. Officials explained this as an order—that the missionaries must not preach to the Indian people, distribute pamphlets, try to convert natives, or allow their converts to do any of these things.

Carey enlisted the help of friends in high places to moderate this order. The missionaries would be allowed to continue their work in Serampore, circulate the scriptures generally, and hold services in private homes of Calcutta—but not in their main house of worship in the city. Natives could preach wherever they wished, provided they were not sent out by Serampore missionaries.

Despite the restrictions placed on the two new missionaries in Calcutta, Carey conducted them and their families to Serampore. The chief of police and the governor-general's office protested, but the new governor of Serampore, Colonel Jacob Krefting, refused to surrender the missionaries. He declared that they were under the special protection of the king of Denmark.

The many foes of missions took heart anew at the coming to India of Lord Gilbert John Minto as governor-general. They presented the matter to him, along with a Serampore pamphlet in Persian that described Muhammed as an "imposter" and "tyrant." Carey had not so much as heard of the pamphlet before, but he was summoned to the office of the governor-general's chief secretary. Carey investigated and discovered that Ward had commissioned a Muslim convert to translate part of a standard work on the Koran. The convert inserted the uncomplimentary terms on his own initiative, and this had escaped Ward's notice during the process of printing.

The missionaries were distressed that such a thing, so out of keeping with their principles of work, had happened. They apologized and withdrew the pamphlet from circulation. Still, Carey received a further order from the authorities that no attempts could be made to convert Bengalis and that the mission press must be transferred to Calcutta.

Carey and Marshman obtained a conference with Lord Minto. They took as a gift to him the part of a classical Hindu writing that Ward had already printed. They explained their mission work to Lord Minto and listed visible results. Approximately one hundred Indians had been baptized, including twelve Brahmins and five Muslims. The missionaries declared that they were prepared to suffer if necessary rather than compromise in regard to their ministries. They added, however, that having to move the presses to Calcutta would mean financial ruin for them, with the high rents and wages that must be paid there.

Lord Minto saw clearly that these men were of entirely different character from what he had been misled to believe. On his initiative, the council of government revoked the previous order and accepted Carey's offer simply to submit all future publications for approval. This would not handicap the missionaries' work, since they had nothing to hide, and government approval might facilitate distribution of their publications in India.

In the meantime, the mental derangement of Carey's wife continued. She tried several times to attack her husband in violence. She died in 1807.

The following year Carey married Charlotte Rumohr, a Danish lady who was practically a lifelong invalid. Naturally weak in constitution, she suffered from a malady of the spine. She had come to India for her health and settled in Serampore at about the same time the mission was established there. A Lutheran by upbringing, she attended the Baptist chapel regularly. She made a profession of faith, and Carey baptized her. This generous lady gave her house to the mission and supported its various projects. The marriage was a particularly happy one both for her and William

Carey. Just after her death in 1821 Carey wrote to Ryland: "My loss is irreparable. I am very lonely."

About sundown on 11 March 1812, after many workers in the Serampore printing plant had gone home, a fire broke out in the south end of the main building, which was two hundred feet long. Ward, still at work in his office at the far end of the building, smelled the smoke. He called for Marshman, as Carey was in Calcutta, and with a few Indians they fought the blaze for hours. They closed all windows and doors and finally brought the fire under control. Then some foolish persons opened windows to throw water through, and the dying embers took on new life. Soon the entire building was in flames.

Ward, Marshman, and the others worked furiously all night fighting the fire and removing what they could. The ruins were still smoking when Carey arrived that evening. The large stock of printing paper was gone as well as untold thousands of printed sheets for Bibles and other works. Even worse was the loss of almost irreplaceable manuscripts of scripture translations, tracts, grammars, dictionaries, and other books—along with about twenty fonts of type in various languages. Carey and Ward estimated the material loss to be at least ten thousand pounds.

Much had been saved—important deeds, records, accounts and five presses the men had been able to carry from the building. The paper mill and warehouse with stocks of printed books did not catch fire. Ward was delighted also to find in the ruins undamaged the punches and matrices with which he could recast type.

When news of the fire reached England, Fuller became a whirlwind of activity in presenting the need. In fifty days he raised the full amount and reported to the mission committee:

> So constantly are the contributions pouring in, from all parties, in and out of the denomination, that I think we must in honesty . . . even stop the contributions.

Within a few weeks after the fire the presses were working again—in another building that belonged to the mission, was rented out, and had just been vacated. In a matter of months all the needed fonts of type had been remade. By the end of the year

Carey was able to write to the society that the mission presses were operating more effectively than ever before.

Freedom for Expansion

The battle for freedom in mission work continued in England. Many military men and former administrative clerks who had served in India maligned the missionaries as disturbers of peace and security. They accused the missionaries of depriving the Indians of their freedom and rights by preaching a religion strange to them, thus undermining their noble indigenous faiths.

The writer Sydney Smith railed, in a paper he published in Scotland, against the "visionary enthusiasts . . . a nest of consecrated cobblers . . . in Bengal." Robert Southey, soon to become poet laureate, answered this condescending critic effectively by citing at length the spiritual and literary accomplishments of the missionaries. William Wilberforce, in the House of Commons, spoke forcefully and at great length in defense of missions. So did Lord Wellesley in the House of Lords; he had been governor-general in India and knew the missionaries well.

Carey wrote to Andrew Fuller suggesting that signatures be gathered all over Britain on petitions to Parliament, and this was done. Fuller wrote extensively and traveled throughout Britain in the campaign. He made innumerable trips to London for consultation with officials of government and the East India Company.

Parliament customarily reconsidered and renewed the company's charter at intervals of twenty years; the time for this came again in 1813. The charter as finally revised reflected the victory of mission supporters. An act of Parliament regarding the people of India stated

> that such measures ought to be adopted as may tend to the introduction among them of useful knowledge and of religious and moral improvement . . . and that facilities shall be afforded, by law, to persons desirous of going and remaining in India, for the purpose of accomplishing these benevolent designs.

The exertions of Fuller in the battle for the right of mission in India, along with his strenuous travel to recoup Serampore's losses in the fire, took their toll. He died in May 1815.

Carey and his colleagues often discussed the need for a college at Serampore—especially to provide higher education for prospective ministers and young people from the churches, but for others also. They sent out the first prospectus in July 1818 and opened the institution as soon as they could after that date. They set no religious requirements for students. The missionaries made ultimate concession in order to help as many as possible and provided for caste distinctions in the dining hall and elsewhere whenever this was insisted upon. There was a small board of trustees, one member of which could be a non-Baptist; Carey was principal of the college.

Lord Francis Moira, who became the Marquis of Hastings, was the new governor-general. He and his wife were generous supporters of the college. The Danish governor of Serampore accepted the honorary position of "first governor of the college" and gave liberally to it.

The college began operation with thirty-seven students: nineteen Indian Christians, fourteen Hindus, and four "having neither caste nor religion." Students in the theological department took general subjects also. Carey did not believe in the segregation of future ministers in a separate theological seminary.

A large and stately building was erected for the college. Including furnishings, the cost was 15,000 pounds, most of which was provided by the Serampore mission and patrons in India. A letter of appreciation and support came from the king of Denmark, who later granted a royal charter empowering the college to grant degrees. The enrollment grew in following years to 100 students—and more recently to 2,000 with 70 in the theological department. Although Britain purchased the Serampore area in 1845 and it later became a part of independent India, the college is said to be the only institution in India with authority to grant degrees in theology.

Krishna Pal, the first Indian convert and a tireless evangelist, died of cholera in August 1822. A few months after this, Felix Carey died of liver disease at the age of thirty-seven. He had given up mission work in 1814, lived a wild and wandering life for several years, then was lured back to Serampore by William Ward. Ward, talented in understanding and helping young people, was spiritual father to all four Carey boys and won them to Christ. Felix, in his last years, helped his father expertly in the preparation of translations for the press. Ignatius Fernandez, faithful businessman-missionary, came to Serampore to die, leaving a church of eighty members in Dinajpur.

The great Serampore Trio was broken in 1823, when William Ward died at the age of fifty-four, within thirty-six hours after the onslaught of cholera.

Carey married Grace Hughes, who like him had been twice widowed, in 1823. This was a happy union. Grace Carey cared for him tenderly in his declining years and survived him by a year.

Not long after his last marriage Carey had a bad fall at the Serampore landing after he had returned by boat at about midnight from a preaching appointment in Calcutta. He had to be carried to his home. High fever developed, and 110 leeches were applied to his thigh to reduce swelling. Carey was unable to walk for three months, then for three more months he used crutches. Pain continued, and he was somewhat handicapped in his movements the remainder of his days.

Carey's second son, William, served the mission well, mainly in Dinajpur and Katwa, which were north of Serampore. Jabez, the third son, was educator and missionary, first in Amboyna (Indonesia) and later in India. Jonathan, the youngest, became a supreme court attorney in Calcutta. He gave generous support to the Serampore mission, served as its treasurer, and was active as a lay preacher.

Benefitting the Country

A barbarous custom that had burdened Carey from the first in India was infanticide. Small children were frequently offered as a sacrifice to the river goddess or left in the jungle to die because they were sickly. George Udney, a member of the governor-general's council in Calcutta, laid the problem before Lord Wellesley, who chose Carey to make an investigation.

With his usual thoroughness, Carey researched and surveyed until he had the pertinent facts. He then reported to the governor-general that the practices were not enjoined in Hindu sacred books. Lord Wellesley then issued an edict declaring that infanticide was murder and that those who committed it would be liable to the death penalty. Soon no more infanticide could be discovered.

While traveling with the indigo business and in evangelism, Carey had observed with horror the practice of *sati*, the burning of a widow fastened on the funeral pyre of her husband. Every time he saw it he protested loudly and vehemently, but relatives insisted that it was the widow's desire.

Carey made widespread investigation of this evil custom, sending researchers into every village within thirty miles of Calcutta. They gathered data as to how many widows had been sacrificed during the preceding year, their ages (some were mere girls), and the number of children left behind. Carey reported that 430 widows had been put to death in this manner during that year. He also pointed out that *sati* had not been generally practiced until comparatively recent times. Although the sacred books commended it as meritorious on the part of the widow, it was nowhere required for Hindu piety.

Lord Wellesley was pleased with the report and seemed ready to take action, but he had been dismissed from his high office and was on the point of departing from India. He felt it appropriate to leave decision on this matter to his successor. He had several successors in the period following his administration, however, and no action was taken.

Lord William Bentinck was governor-general when an order reached Carey, as official government translator, just as he prepared to enter the pulpit Sunday, 6 December 1829. A glance at the document showed that it was the answer to his prayers and efforts across the years, a proclamation declaring *sati* to be a criminal offense. Carey would not risk the loss of more lives by delay. He turned the pulpit over to another person for that day, called for his pundit, and sat down to the painstaking task of making an exact translation into Bengali. By evening the task was finished, and the lifesaving proclamation went out over the land.

Brahmins made an uproar and sent an appeal even to the king in Britain, but Lord Bentinck held his ground, and the memorable action was sustained. Faced with a probable charge of murder if nearest relatives committed *sati*, they quickly learned to live with the new law.

As a part of the government's economy measures, Fort William College was changed in 1831 from a teaching school to simply an examining body. Professor Carey was retired on a rather good pension, which went to the mission fund in Serampore, as did other income. With the school's change in status, he could add courses in theology and botany to his teaching at Serampore College. He preached regularly in Bengali and English. He continued translation work and completed his final revision of the Bengali Bible. To Marshman, his devoted fellow-laborer of so many years, Carey said, "I have not a single desire ungratified."

Carey never did return to England. Sad divisions might have been averted if he had taken furloughs. He always felt that the work in India required his unceasing attention—personal evangelism, counseling with inquirers, preaching, teaching, and especially Bible translation. He never even took a vacation from his labors.

He had a garden, however, everywhere he lived, in England and in India. He liked to spend an hour or two each morning and again in the evening working and praying in his splendid five-acre garden in Serampore. Professional botanists estimated it to be one of the best in the East. Each kind of plant was posted with its classical botanical name. Carey had continually asked his correspondents in Britain, America, and the East to send him seeds and plants from their areas. He developed new species in India and even had a flower named for him. The five-acre Serampore garden had to be replanted several times—after a widespread flood, after a devastating cyclone, and after the garden part of the property was taken for other uses by the mission society in London.

A botanist in England sent a bag of seeds to Carey, who wrote the donor later:

> That I might be sure not to lose any part of your valuable present, I shook the bag over a patch of earth in a shady place: on visiting which a few days afterwards I found springing up, to my inexpressible delight, a *Bellis perennis* of our English pastures. I know not that I ever enjoyed,

since leaving Europe, a simple pleasure so exquisite as the sight of this
English Daisy afforded me; not having seen one for upwards of thirty
years, and never expecting to see one again.

Carey led in the formation of the Agri-horticultural Society of
India and served for a time as its president. He belonged to the
Asiatic Society of Bengal, the Geological Society, and the Linnean
Society of London. He was a corresponding member of the Royal
Horticultural Society.

The Sadness of Separation

Relationships with the mission society in England were never the
same after Fuller died. Pearce and Sutcliff had passed on before
him. Of the original group of supporters who had known Carey
personally, only Ryland remained. He was principal of Bristol College, which trained Baptist ministers, and did not have time to take
a leading part in the direction of the mission during the remaining
decade of his life.

John Dyer came increasingly into leadership and became general secretary about two years after Fuller's death. The managing
committee was greatly enlarged. Many of the members were unsympathetic with much of the work in Serampore, especially the
college after it was established. Dyer and others wanted to organize everything on a businesslike basis. They attempted to put new
measures into effect with bureaucratic rigidity and little understanding of the situation.

The India mission had been largely self-supporting. If it had
been otherwise in the early years, the missionaries would not have
had food for their families. Self-support was a goal Carey adopted
from the Moravians. He desired that available funds go to the establishment of new missions throughout the non-Christian world.

Carey wrote to Ryland in 1817 that all funds sent to India by
the society since the beginning, including the ten thousand pounds
for rebuilding after the fire, would not have been more than
enough to provide a modest living allowance for each missionary
family there. It has been estimated by another that in all Carey's
life he personally received less than six hundred pounds from the
mission society, while he contributed from his earnings about forty

thousand pounds to the Baptist work in India. The Serampore mission developed and supported, mainly in Bengal, as many as sixteen or more churches and missions.

The mission society's managing committee, by 1817 based in London, demanded a statement of all accounts in Serampore. The missionaries had always scrupulously reported to the society all expenditures on amounts received from it, but not on their own earnings and gifts from friends in India and America. The committee in London demanded not only control over expenditures but management of all property and equipment by a board of trustees, five members of which would be in England and three in Serampore—and this when it still took several months for a letter to travel each way. The missionaries never claimed any of the property as theirs. They simply felt they knew the needs and resources and could manage things better on the field.

Rumors circulated, in the committee and among Baptist generally, that the missionaries lived in luxury and that each family had accumulated a private fortune. Nothing could of course be further from the truth. They were poor while they lived and poor when they died.

Reorganization was in order. Mission societies in Europe and America had developed somewhat standardized principles of work, but there were no principles but Carey's when he and Thomas went into mission work. What hurt the Serampore missionaries most was the way in which changes were to be brought about and the spirit in which they were done. Carey complained that whereas he had always corresponded with Fuller and other supporters as brethren, the letters from Dyer seemed like official statements from a secretary of state.

A further sadness was division of forces on the field. More missionaries were leaving, since British law protected them in doing so. Among new Baptist missionaries were a son of the late dearly beloved Samuel Pearce and also Carey's own nephew, Eustace Carey. Serampore mission stations were in crying need of workers, and the senior missionaries begged the new ones to go to these places.

Instead, five new mission families—including the Eustace Careys—separated from Serampore and established a competing mission in Calcutta, where there were churches and preaching stations already. The new group members, none of them over twenty-six years of age, opened chapels in Calcutta and the surrounding areas, set up a printing press, and started schools. They placed themselves explicitly under the direct supervision of the committee in London, received allowances from it for living expenses, and gave their own secular earnings as funds for the society.

Opposition centered on Marshman, whom the young missionaries regarded as arbitrary. They blamed him for unnecessary expenditures, for seeking special favors for his children, and even for exercising undue influence on Ward and Carey. Only the inclination "to display his children to advantage" did Carey admit in any sense to be true and that to an insignificant degree. "I wish I had half his piety, energy of mind, and zeal for the cause of God," Carey wrote. The new missionaries invited Carey to join them, but they refused to work with Marshman.

In a letter to Christopher Anderson of Edinburgh, a strong supporter of Serampore to the end, Carey wrote:

> The unworthy attempts . . . to separate Brother Marshman and me are truly contemptible. I intend to continue connected with him and Serampore as long as I live.

Marshman went to London in 1827 in an effort to discuss the problem with the mission committee, hoping to reach an acceptable agreement. The committee refused any compromise and treated Marshman with disrespect. In grief and heaviness of heart he felt obliged somewhat later to sign an "agreement of separation," turning over to the mission committee all the churches and missions sponsored by Serampore and all the properties at Serampore except the college and its grounds. (Many committee members opposed the college.) The separation lasted many years. Carey spent the remainder of his life outside the mission society he had founded, as did his faithful co-worker Marshman. Serampore College eventually became independent.

Man of Vision

In Carey's final months Lord and Lady Bentinck visited him. The Anglican bishop of Calcutta knelt at his bedside to receive the old man's blessing. Alexander Duff, young Church of Scotland missionary, visited often for counsel and fellowship.

Duff was one of the last visitors. He spoke on this occasion with much appreciation of the veteran's contributions in mission service. Then Carey whispered, "Pray." Duff knelt and prayed. Then as Duff was leaving the room he thought he heard a feeble voice whispering his name. He stepped back to the dying man, who said, "Mr. Duff, you have been speaking about Dr. Carey, Dr. Carey. When I am gone, say nothing about Dr. Carey—speak about Dr. Carey's Saviour."

William Carey died 9 June 1834, at the age of seventy-two. His body was laid beside the grave of his second wife, Charlotte. The Danish flag flew at half mast in Serampore. The governor of the little colony and his wife stood at the graveside for the final service, along with national Christians, Hindus, and Muslims. Calcutta newspapers extolled Carey as a great linguist and missionary. In accordance with his request the gravestone bore simply his name, dates of birth and death, and the words of Isaac Watts's hymn:

> A wretched, poor and helpless worm,
> on thy kind arms I fall.

A bust of Carey was placed at a prominent place in the horticultural gardens of Calcutta and an avenue in the botanical gardens named for him. A tablet was placed in his memory in the chancel of Paulerspury parish church in England, and a beautiful lectern in Westminister Abbey bore the inscription:

> Expect Great Things from God:
> Attempt Great Things for God.

In the *Enquiry* Carey had envisioned the organization of additional mission societies, and these came into being rather rapidly. The Congregationalists' London Missionary Society was first, in

1795. Other societies of various Protestant groups soon followed—in Scotland, the Netherlands, England, Germany, Switzerland, and the U.S.A.

At the beginning of his missionary career Carey's plans were modest, but he learned to think in large terms, considering that nothing less was worthy of those in kingdom service. "I feel a burning desire," he said, "that all the world may know." His plans for rapid expansion of evangelistic and church-building efforts in India caused uneasiness among home supporters. As the Baptist society was planning retrenchment in Java and Ceylon, Carey wrote:

> Considering the extensive countries opened to us in the east, I entreat, I implore, our dear brethren in England not to think of the petty shop-keeping plan of lessening the number of stations so as to bring the support of them within the bounds of their present income, but bend all their attention and exertions to the great object of increasing their finances, to meet the pressing demand that divine Providence makes on them. If your objects are large, the public will contribute to their support; if you contract them their liberality will immediately contract itself proportionately.

In a letter to Fuller, Carey suggested the holding of international mission conferences about every ten years, beginning perhaps at the Cape of Good Hope in 1810. Mission and church workers would understand each other better in two hours at such a gathering, Carey said, than in two years of correspondence. The idea was not a congenial one to Fuller. He called it just one of Carey's pleasing dreams. Many have seen as its fulfillment the great international missionary conferences that began at Edinburgh, Scotland in 1910—just a century late, according to Carey's proposal.

Carey once remarked to his nephew Eustace Carey:

> If, after my removal, anyone should think it worth his while to write my life, I will give you a criterion by which you may judge of its correctness. If he give me credit for being a plodder, he will describe me justly. Anything beyond this will be too much. I can plod. I can persevere in any definite pursuit. To this I owe everything.

Note on Sources

The more recently published biographies of Carey were quite useful in preparation of this present sketch, as were the writer's visits to Carey sites in England and India. Quotations are from the older books listed below. Authors include Joseph Belcher, Eustace Carey, William Carey, J. C. Marshman, and George Smith.

Selected Bibliography

Belcher, Joseph. *William Carey: A Biography*. Philadelphia, n.d.

Carey, Eustace. *Memoir of William Carey, D.D.* London, 1836.

Carey S. Pearce. *William Carey, D.D., Fellow of Linnaean Society*. 4th ed. London: Hodder and Stoughton, 1924.

Carey, S. Pearce. *William Carey*. London: The Carey Press, 1942.

Carey, William. *An Enquiry into the Obligations of Christians to Use Means for the Conversion of the Heathens*. Leicester, England, 1792. New facsimile edition. London: The Carey Kingsgate Press, 1934.

Dakin, A. *William Carey: Shoemaker, Linguist, Missionary*. Nashville TN: Broadman Press, 1942.

Drewery, Mary. *William Carey, A Biography*. Grand Rapids MI: Zondervan Publishing House, 1979.

George, Timothy. *Faithful Witness: The Life and Mission of William Carey*. Birmingham AL: New Hope, 1991.

Marshman, John Clark. *The Story of Carey, Marshman and Ward, the Serampore Missionaries*. Popular edition. London, 1864.

Middlebrook, J. B. *William Carey*. London: The Carey Kingsgate Press, 1961.

Oussoren, A. H. *William Carey, Especially His Missionary Principles*. Leiden: the Netherlands, 1945.

Smith, George. *The Life of William Carey, D.D., Shoemaker and Missionary*. London, 1887.

Walker, F. Deaville. *William Carey, Missionary Pioneer and Statesman*. Chicago: Moody Press, n.d.

Adoniram Judson—
Devoted for Life

Adoniram Judson entered Rhode Island College (Brown University) a few days after his sixteenth birthday and was forthwith admitted to the sophomore class. This did not come as the first indication that he possessed exceptional abilities. His mother had taught him at the age of three to read passages from the Bible. A few years later he amazed teachers and schoolmates by his ability to solve difficult puzzles and mathematical problems. He read avidly in various types of literature and did well in Latin and Greek before reaching his teens.

Adoniram distinguished himself as a university student. He took a leading part in the Philemenian Society's debate and literary activities. Although inclined to introspection, he enjoyed some popularity at campus parties. Of slightly less than average height, he had a round boyish face and a fairly long and pointed nose; but his wavy chestnut-colored hair, flashing brown eyes, cheery smile, and sprightly walk made him a rather attractive young man—even to the ladies.

Among Adoniram's close associates at Brown University were students who later became outstanding leaders, judges, congressmen, cabinet members, and a state governor. His favorite was an upperclassman from Maine, Jacob Eames, an outspoken deist. Persons like Eames acknowledged a creator God but denied that this God had arranged a special incarnate revelation, inspired the writing of sacred books, or intervened in human affairs. The revelation in nature sufficed, the deist said, and reason alone must determine beliefs.

Adoniram idolized the brilliant and witty Jacob Eames and embraced his philosophy of life. Both young men were exceedingly ambitious and often discussed their future work. Literature—especially the writing of plays—attracted them, along with the practice of law, since it might provide opportunities for attaining high public office. Eames finished his studies a year ahead of Judson, who graduated as valedictorian of his class in 1807.

After graduation Adoniram lived in Plymouth, Massachusetts
with his parents, a slightly younger sister, and a brother six years
younger. His father served as the pastor of a very conservative
Congregational church. Adoniram conducted a private school during the year he remained in Plymouth. He also wrote two text-
books on grammar and arithmetic that were published by a firm
in Boston. He attended church and family worship as was expected of him, but he was living a lie and was miserable.

Suddenly, on his twentieth birthday, he closed the school and
announced to the family his intention to travel. This saddened
everyone. His father suggested that if he did not like teaching perhaps he could prepare for the ministry. Adoniram reacted with
indignation and blurted out that, far from being interested in the
ministry, he no longer believed cardinal doctrines of Christianity
such as an authoritative Bible and the deity of Christ. Pastor Judson was horrified and tried to debate with his son. The latter had
no difficulty in demolishing his father's arguments logically, but
he could find no effective rebuttal for his mother's tears.

Quest For Freedom

It was an unhappy parting as Adoniram rode away on his horse.
He journeyed first to Boston, then 150 miles across the state to
Sheffield, where his elderly uncle served as pastor. Leaving the
horse with his uncle, he took passage down the Hudson River to
New York City on the recently developed steamboat, the *Clermont*.
(Adoniram decided to use the name "Johnson"—sometimes a mis-
understanding of "Judson"—during the period of adventures he
anticipated. This could save his parents embarrassment in case
negative reports somehow reached them.)

In New York, reflecting on the plans he and Jacob Eames had
discussed about writing plays, he joined a disreputable traveling
group of players—not as an actor but just to familiarize himself
with the medium. With this troupe he led, as he later described it,
"a reckless, vagabond life, finding lodgings where we could, and
bilking the landlord where we found opportunity—in other words,
running up a score, and then decamping without paying the rec-
koning." (After his conversion, he retraced the route taken with the

troupe and paid his evaded obligations.) Disgusted with the players' lifestyle and gaining no useful experience, Adoniram left the group one night without notice.

He returned to Sheffield for his horse then headed again westward. That evening he stopped at a village inn. The innkeeper mentioned as he led him to his room that since the place was almost fully occupied, he would have to place "Mr. Johnson" next door to a young man who was very ill, perhaps dying. Adoniram confidently assured the innkeeper that this would cause him no uneasiness at all—but it did.

Sounds came from the sickroom—groans of the sufferer and movements and voices of those attending him. The most troublesome of all were Adoniram's thoughts. The innkeeper had said this was a young man and that he might be dying. Was he prepared? Adoniram felt a blush of shame at the thought, for it revealed to him the shallowness of his deistic philosophy. He wondered what his recent companions would say to such intellectual and emotional weakness as he was experiencing. What would the brilliant and bold Jacob Eames say?

The restless night continued. Although he fought within himself against it, Adoniram's thoughts reverted incessantly to the sick man. Was he a Christian, strong and at peace in his soul, or did he shudder on the brink of a fearsome and hopeless afterlife? Adoniram imagined himself in that sickbed and wondered what his own eternal fate would be.

Finally, morning came. The sunlight dispelled what he felt were superstitious illusions of the night. After he arose and washed, he went to find the innkeeper and inquire about the condition of his sick neighbor.

"He is dead," said the innkeeper.

"Dead!"

"Yes, he is gone, poor fellow. The doctor said he would probably not survive the night."

"Do you know who he was?" Adoniram inquired.

"Oh, yes," replied the innkeeper. "It was a young man from Providence College, a very fine fellow. His name was Jacob Eames."

Adoniram went into shock. His later recollection of this time remained hazy, and he did not like to speak of it. So far as can be determined, he never gave to anyone the details—whether he revealed his connection with the deceased, got in touch with the latter's relatives, viewed the body, or made any arrangements. One may wonder whether Eames had relatives in the vicinity, but apparently no informative records have been found.

After several hours had passed, somehow, he mechanically mounted his horse and resumed the journey westward. Troubling thoughts still thundered in his brain—Jake Eames was dead. Deep down, he sensed biblical religion to be true, and he was in despair for himself. Suddenly, as he disconsolately rode westward, he resolved to abandon his travel plans. He turned the horse around and headed toward Plymouth. The family rejoiced at Adoniram's return home and his evident change in attitudes, but he remained extremely unsettled.

After a few weeks he accepted an invitation to enroll as a special student in a new conservative seminary at Andover, just northwest of Boston. The classification as "special" seemed necessary because Adoniram had not yet made a profession of faith, much less a decision for the ministry. Again, as in college, he was admitted to second-year studies.

Finding a Life Mission

Adoniram applied himself diligently, studying the Bible in its original languages and holding long discussions with the seminary's two professors about his theological problems. Within a month he began to see the light. On 2 December 1808, he made what he called a solemn dedication of himself to God. Later he stated publicly his profession of faith and joined Pastor Judson's Congregational Church in Plymouth.

Brown University offered Adoniram a tutorship but he declined it. He began to have some intimation of what his future life might be like when he read a printed sermon about needs in India written by a former British chaplain in that land. This implanted in his mind the challenge of taking the gospel to distant peoples. A few missionaries had gone from Europe, including the English

Baptist William Carey. So far as Adoniram knew, no American had considered such a thing. He read all he could find on the subject. One book that fascinated him was a British officer's account of a diplomatic mission to Burma. From that time on, Burma was never far from his thoughts.

On a cold day in January 1810, the commitment came—as Judson described it long afterward:

> It was during a solitary walk in the woods behind the college, while meditating and praying on the subject and feeling half inclined to give it up, that the command of Christ, "Go into all the world, and preach the gospel to every creature," was presented in my mind with such clearness and power that I came to a full decision and—though great difficulties appeared in my way—resolved to obey the command at all events.

Soon afterward Adoniram went home to Plymouth for the winter vacation. There he received news of an invitation to become assistant pastor of "the largest church in Boston." The elder Judson congratulated his son enthusiastically. His mother added, "and you will be so near home." Soon his sister joined in, and he could stand it no longer. He knew his father's high ambitions for him, and he had dreaded breaking the news on his own decision. He knew he must. He directed his statement to Abby, the last one who had spoken.

No sister," he said, "I shall never live in Boston. I would much farther than that to go." He proceeded to summarize his hopes and plans. His beloved family, although shocked, did not presume to offer strong opposition. They knew that if Adoniram had made up his mind, there was no changing his decision.

Back at Andover, Adoniram found to his surprise that at least four other students were dealing with the challenge of Christian mission. One of the young men, Samuel Mills, had transferred from the theological school at Yale. Almost four years earlier, while studying at Williams College, Mills had led several fellow students in the "haystack prayer meeting" to commit themselves to mission work.

Later, at Williams College, Mills led in organizing the Society of Brethren, a small and secret group of men committed to keep themselves free to go out as missionaries whenever the way should be opened. The Society of Brethren set up its volunteer band at Andover. Soon two other members came from Williams, including Luther Rice. Some students became interested in mission work among American Indians, but most of the volunteers apparently still hoped for a foreign mission.

They agreed that all of their efforts at the time should focus on finding a way for the three seniors of their number—Adoniram Judson, Samuel Nott, and Samuel Newell—to be sent to the mission field. Adoniram and one of the seminary professors wrote to the London Missionary Society, which had been organized mainly by Congregationalists in 1795, to ask whether it would appoint them as its missionaries. Meanwhile the volunteers, with Mills in the lead, promoted the idea of mission support in American churches.

A new organization for evangelical Congregationalists in Massachusetts was scheduled to convene in Bradford on 28 June 1810. After conferring with their professors and other ministers, the volunteers asked Adoniram to prepare a statement for presentation at the meeting. Association leaders agreed to place this on the agenda for the afternoon session the first day. Only four students—the three seniors and Mills—signed the statement for fear of alarming the church fathers by too large a number seeking support. These four persons and three other volunteers walked the ten miles to Bradford that morning then back again that evening. Adoniram had been chosen also to read the statement to the assembly.

There were nineteen delegates and nine guests—all ministers— on the main floor of the church where the meeting was held. At the afternoon session, the four students who had signed the statement were ushered to the front pew. The other three students crammed into the crowded balcony. When the moderator called for this item of business, Adoniram stepped forward and read in his clear resonant voice:

> The undersigned . . . beg leave to state that their minds have been long impressed with the duty and importance of personally attempting a mission to the heathen; . . . and after examining all the information that they can obtain, they consider themselves devoted to this work for life, wherever God, in his providence, shall open the way.

The statement recognized difficulties and asked whether the students should give up the project as impracticable, concentrate their mission efforts in the homeland, seek support from a European society, or expect support from a mission society in America.

Each of the four students gave a brief testimony about his decision for mission service. The moderator appointed a committee to consider the matter and report to the association delegates the next day.

In its report the committee suggested that the offer of the students be affirmed and

> that there be instituted, by this general association, a board of commissioners for foreign missions, for the purpose of devising ways and means, and adopting and prosecuting measures, for promoting the spread of the gospel in heathen lands.

This report, which the association adopted, also advised the student volunteers to put themselves

> under the patronage and direction of the Board of Commissioners for Foreign Missions, humbly to wait the openings and guidance of providence in respect to their great and excellent design.

The association named members from Connecticut also on the "American Board," as this first foreign mission sending agency in the United States was already called. Gradually it became a national organization for Congregationalists.

Another Mission in Bradford

Between the hikes of the students to and from Bradford on that summer's day in 1810, Adoniram began a second "mission." He and other associational participants went to the spacious home of deacon John Hasseltine for the noon meal. There he met Ann, the deacon's youngest daughter, who helped to serve the guests. Nancy, as she was often called by her friends, was a sprightly, black-haired beauty of twenty years. Adoniram thought he had never met such a charming person.

Ann had felt considerable excitement in looking forward to seeing this young man who had created such a stir about missions. When she did meet him, however, she was rather disappointed. He seemed shy and retiring, avoiding as much as possible any part in conversation. He answered direct questions with uninspired brevity. Perhaps he felt nervous about the presentation he was to make to the association that afternoon. In any case, he seemed to keep his eyes fixed on the dinner plate before him. Ann did not know until much later that he was engaged in trying to compose in his mind a poem to Ann Hasseltine, the loveliest girl he had ever seen.

Ann grew up with three older sisters and a brother. Intelligent and high-spirited, she was the pet of her family and popular around town. She attended Bradford Academy and ranked high as a student. In her early teens her life revolved primarily about balls and parties, many of which took place at the Hasseltine home in the second-floor "frolic room"—or as critics dubbed it, the "Hasseltine Dance Hall."

At age fifteen Ann was influenced by the devotional talks of a dedicated principal at Bradford Academy and the reading of inspirational books. She battled in spirit with the issue for several months, then made a surrender of her life to Christ on the evening of 6 July 1806. From that time on she led an exemplary Christian life and influenced members of her family, including her fun-loving father, to do the same.

After attending Bradford Academy, she taught school for several years, seeking always the spiritual as well as the intellectual advancement of her pupils. Despite her new seriousness, Ann had lost none of her vivacity and charm when Adoniram met her. It is no wonder that for him it was love at first sight. Not long afterward he wrote to her indicating, rather clearly, his desire that she become his wife. Ann delayed her reply and then wrote evasively that her parents must give their consent and that she questioned whether she could be sufficiently committed to God to face the uncertain future of a missionary's wife. In the same writing she came to the conclusion: "Yes, I feel willing to be placed in this situation, in which I can do most good, though it were to carry the Gospel to the distant, benighted heathen."

Adoniram wrote to Ann's father:

> I have now to ask whether you can consent to part with your
> daughter early next spring, to see her no more in this world
> whether you can consent to her departure to a heathen land,
> and her subjection to the hardships and sufferings of a mission-
> ary life . . . to the fatal influence of the climate of India; to
> every kind of want and distress; to degradation, insult, persecu-
> tion, and perhaps a violent death . . . for the sake of Him who
> left his heavenly home, and died for her and for you, for the
> sake of perishing, immortal souls . . . and the glory of God?

Ann's parents, although deeply troubled at the thought of losing their beloved Ann, bravely left the decision to her. She sought
counsel from relatives and friends. She still doubted sometimes
that she would have the spiritual stamina for mission work on a
foreign field. Gradually she seemed to partake of Adoniram's
strength and self-assurance. He kept in frequent communication
with her and visited Bradford as often as he could to expedite the
courtship. The young couple took horseback rides together over
the countryside. Within a month or two the matter seemed to be
generally regarded as settled that Ann Hasseltine would marry Mr.
Judson and go with him for missionary service in Eastern lands.

In the meantime Judson continued to prepare for his anticipated work. He graduated from Andover seminary on 24 September,
nineteen days after his alma mater—Brown University—awarded
him the master of arts degree. Earlier in the year he had been
licensed to the ministry, and he preached in churches in the
Andover vicinity after graduation.

Soon Judson received a positive reply on appointment from the
London Missionary Society. By that time, however, there seemed
to be some hope of support from American Congregationalists,
though adequate funding failed. The American Board had been
able to raise only a few hundred dollars. It decided, therefore, to
send Judson to confer with the London Missionary Society and
find out whether this society would cooperate with the American
Board in support of the candidates. Friends advanced funds for
Judson's overseas trip, and the board promised to reimburse them
later.

Hijacked on the High Seas

Judson sailed on the *Packet*, a British freighter, on 11 January 1811. The only other passengers were two Spanish merchants. After three weeks, two French privateers captured the *Packet*, for France and England were at war. The merchants received good treatment because they could speak French and place bribes effectively, but Judson was thrown into the hold with the British sailors who were prisoners of war.

Unable to communicate with his captors, angered at being treated like a common criminal, and repelled by the filth and stench about him, Adoniram languished in misery in the darkness. For the first time, he seemed to have doubts about his chosen course and whether he had acted wisely in turning down that invitation to be assistant pastor in "the largest church in Boston."

His spirits had definitely hit bottom, but for him the bounce back was inevitable. He began to pray and felt God might be using this disagreeable experience to prepare him for trials later in missionary service. He determined to stop feeling sorry for himself and looked for some useful activity.

Fumbling in his travel bag, Judson found his Hebrew Bible and began to read it. As a mental exercise, he translated it into Latin as he read. The ship's doctor, seeing the book in some strange language, realized this was not an ordinary seaman. He addressed Judson in Latin and was answered with enthusiasm in that language. The captive explained that he was an American passenger on the British vessel. The doctor arranged for him to be given a berth on the upper deck and a place at the captain's table with the Spanish merchants.

The latter freely disembarked on the Spanish coast, but all of the others from the *Packet* were taken to Bayonne, France. There, to his dismay, Judson was again thrown with members of the British crew and marched through the city. Attempting to use the few words of French he had learned, he protested loudly at the treatment he received. This brought only threats from guards and laughs from passersby. Then he yelled out in English his denunciation of oppression in general and the present outrage in particular.

Finally, a tall man came from the crowd and walked beside him. He told Judson to lower his voice or he would bring greater punishment on himself. Adoniram quickly explained his situation. The man said he was an American and would help, then quickly disappeared again into the crowd.

The captives were taken to a massive, gloomy-looking prison and thrown into a dark, musty, underground room with straw around the walls. The other prisoners chose places and lay down, but Judson refused even to sit on the filthy straw, pacing instead all about the room. He wondered whether the American would really do anything to help him.

After what seemed like hours, he noticed the tall man being admitted by the jailor. Adoniram suppressed a shout of thankfulness when he noticed that the man carefully avoided looking at him.

"Let me see if I know any of these poor fellows," he mused aloud, taking a lamp and passing around the room, looking at the various prisoners. "No, no friend of mine," he declared, putting the lamp back into its place. Then quickly he flung his huge military cloak over the slight figure of Adoniram and walked swiftly with him out of the place, putting money into the hand of the jailor as he passed. A further bribe went to the guard at the gate.

Outside, the American friend released Adoniram and whispered hoarsely to him, "Now run!" The long-legged man led the way, but Adoniram followed close behind as they raced through the streets. When they reached a safe place to talk, the tall man explained that he hailed from Philadelphia and was an officer on one of the American ships trying to run the British blockade. He placed Adoniram in the attic of the house of an acquaintance where he stayed until the rescuer was able to arrange parole papers. Adoniram found a room in the boarding house of an American lady who was a long-time resident of France. There he remained six weeks, awaiting a permit to proceed to England.

Adoniram wanted to learn something of French society and for this purpose attended various places of entertainment, the last of which featured a masked ball. Shocked at the goings-on, he called out in English for attention and delivered what amounted to a sermon denouncing such an empty and depraved manner of life. He enumerated evils that infidelity had allegedly brought on France and the world, reflecting no doubt on his own earlier wanderings in French deism. He appealed to his hearers to forsake this worldly life and give themselves to the Christian way. Many had obviously understood what he said. The maskers stood respectfully aside as he marched from the place.

Launching the Mission Enterprise

After receiving his travel papers, Judson proceeded to England. He was cordially received by directors of the London Missionary Society. Three weeks elapsed before the society reached a decision on the query from the American Board regarding possible collaboration in sending out American missionaries. Judson had conferences with a committee appointed to discuss the matter with him.

During this time he visited churches in and around London. He was still quite youthful in appearance, ruddy-faced and delicate-looking—but he had a manly voice. After he had preached in a London pulpit the pastor spoke of the young American's proposed mission to the East, then added, "And if his faith is proportioned to his voice, he will drive the devil from all India."

The LMS expressed no interest in the question of joint administration and support. The two groups could not meet together, and it took a month or more for a letter to cross the Atlantic. Tense relations between the two countries suggested that communications might be broken at any time. Judson confessed that prospects for considerable participation of the American churches in financial support seemed unlikely.

Not one to equivocate when the issue became clear, and being primarily concerned that he and the others be sent out as soon as possible, Judson offered himself to the LMS—along with Nott, Newell, and Hall if they agreed. His only stipulations were that they be assigned to a mission somewhere together and that they be allowed to marry and take their wives. The LMS approved the four for appointment.

This business concluded, Adoniram visited the missionary training school in Gosport, England. He sailed on 18 June and arrived in New York seven weeks later.

At the next meeting of the American Board, several members expressed dissatisfaction regarding Judson's conduct with the London Missionary Society. He had obviously not urged the matter of joint administration and support. Some persons suggested that he be disqualified for mission service. The board's financial outlook seemed bleak. A rich couple had left a bequest of $30,000 to it, but the will was challenged and these funds would probably not be available for a long time, if ever.

War with Britain seemed imminent to the mission candidates and many others. Judson and Nott pressed the American Board to send them out right away, or they would turn to the LMS. The president of the board and others called this an ultimatum and resented it greatly. They opposed hasty action and had a resolution passed by the board issuing a formal reprimand to Judson for not following instructions in dealings with the LMS.

Swallowing their pride and mustering their courage, however, the commissioners voted on 18 September 1811

> that this board do not advise Messrs. Adoniram Judson, jun., and Samuel Nott, jun., to place themselves at present under the direction of the London Missionary Society.

These two men, along with Samuel Newell and Gordon Hall (Hall being considered by the Brethren group as more suitable than Mills for foreign service), were "appointed missionaries to labor under the direction of this board in Asia." Salaries were fixed at $666.66 a year for a couple and somewhat less for a single missionary.

The American Board was again pressured by circumstances. The situation with Britain worsened still further, and New York harbor was already blockaded. No ships seemed to be leaving from U.S. ports for East Asia. Then Newell and Hall suddenly appeared with the news that the *Harmony* would be sailing from Philadelphia for Calcutta in about two weeks. The mission board borrowed money and made arrangements for the missionaries' passage on that vessel and the *Caravan*, for which announcement came a few days later. Owners of both ships had to secure sailing permission from the federal government.

Adoniram had an intense dislike of farewells. He slipped away from home early on the morning of 3 February without awakening his parents and Abby to say goodbye. His brother Elnathan, then eighteen, rode with him as far as Boston. Adoniram felt burdened that his brother had never made a profession of faith, and he spoke with him about it as they rode along together. At one point, they dismounted and knelt by the side of the road. Adoniram voiced a prayer for his brother's salvation, but the missionary never received assurance from him that this had become a reality.

Ann and Adoniram were married by the Bradford pastor on 5 February at the Hasseltine home, in the same room where they had first met. Samuel Newell married Harriett Atwood, not yet seventeen, a very close friend of Ann's. Samuel Nott married on 8 February.

Adoniram's plan for leave-taking in Bradford was about the same as it had been in Plymouth, but it did not work. He hurried Ann off before dawn without giving her a chance to say goodbye to anyone. Their departure was soon detected, however. They were chased down and brought back for farewells.

The five men missionaries received ordination on 6 February in an impressive and emotion-packed service at Tabernacle Church in Salem, Massachusetts. The Judsons and Newells sailed from the port there on the *Caravan*, and the others from Philadelphia sailed five days later.

Dealing with a Troublesome Question

The *Caravan* was the first command of Augustine Heard, only twenty-seven years of age, but he proved himself an able and considerate captain. In the days before refrigeration, diet could be a serious problem on long sea voyages, but Captain Heard had made provision. Pens of grunting pigs and coops of chickens evidenced his foresight for the meat supply.

Getting needed exercise required ingenuity by the missionaries. The vessel measured only ninety feet from stem to stern. With all the coops and pens on deck, the passengers had difficulty taking a brisk walk. For a time they tried rope-jumping. Then they decided dancing would be more enjoyable, but for this exercise they remained in their cabins.

The *Caravan* landed at Calcutta on 17 June 1812. The two missionary couples accepted the hospitality offered by the British Baptist missionaries in Serampore, a tiny Danish province near Calcutta. The plan was for the American missionaries to proceed as soon as possible to Burma and begin their mission work, though all persons with whom they spoke about it strongly advised against it. These advisors described the Burmese "emperor" as an absolute despot who regarded all subjects as his slaves and would surely not tolerate any Burmese leaving the Buddhist faith. The few persons who had tried to do this generally suffered torture or death.

Beginning in 1807 the Serampore group had attempted to conduct a mission in Burma. Of the four missionaries who had gone there, one had died and two had given up and left. The London Missionary Society had sent a mission of two men; one died and the other left within a year. There were no converts. A Portuguese Roman Catholic priest resided in Rangoon, but he served only among Portuguese descendants.

Felix Carey, son of the veteran missionary in Serampore, still resided as a "missionary" in Rangoon. He did a little translation work but never preached to Burmese. He was apparently allowed to remain in the country because no one knew him as a missionary, he had married a Burmese woman, and he gave himself more and more to diplomatic service under the Burmese king—the so-called emperor.

Finally persuaded that Burma probably could not be their field of service at the time, the Judsons and Newells considered India, which seemed just as impossible. The earliest British Baptist missionaries had been forced to take refuge in little Serampore. The British East India Company not only conducted business in India but in effect ruled it also. It regarded the propagation of any new religion in its territories as a disturbing and dangerous factor. American missionaries were even less welcome than the British. War had already been declared between the U.S. and Britain, but news of this had not yet reached India.

Searching for a place to go, the Judsons and Newells finally obtained permits to proceed to the Isle of France (Mauritius), east of Madagascar, under British rule but not administered by the East India Company. The only ship bound for the Isle of France, however, could take only two passengers. Harriett Newell was far advanced in pregnancy, and all agreed that the Newells should take the two places so that they could be settled by the time the baby came.

A British couple in Calcutta invited the Judsons to reside with them while they awaited passage to the Isle of France. The wife's late husband had been a British Baptist missionary, and his library contained a number of books on baptism, which Judson studied in an attempt to settle his own questions on the subject. He had already reached the point where he felt he could not conscientiously fulfill the "instructions" issued by the American Board to missionaries that they should baptize the children and servants of all who become Christians in a pagan land.

Ann still resisted, saying, "If you become a Baptist, I will not." She studied the subject anyway, and soon they found themselves in complete agreement on the question.

The "Serampore Trio"—Carey, Joshua Marshman, and William Ward—was astounded at the end of August to receive a letter from the Judsons asking for baptism. Ward baptized Adoniram and Ann in the Lal Bazar Chapel in Calcutta on 6 September. Shortly thereafter Judson preached in the same chapel a sermon on baptism that William Carey declared to be the best he had ever heard on the subject. This sermon was printed in Serampore and in Boston.

The Judsons stood alone, receiving no further support from the American Board. The separation from their erstwhile missionary colleagues caused them much grief. The Serampore mission advanced funds as needed. Judson recalled that in a brief conversation with the Baptist Dr. Lucius Bolles of Salem before embarkation, he had suggested that Baptists in America should also form a society for foreign missions. Judson had no idea at the time that he would ever be involved in such an enterprise. Later he wrote to both Dr. Bolles and a leading Baptist pastor in Boston and offered himself as a missionary of their denomination if this were desired.

The *Harmony* reached Calcutta four days after the Newells had left for the Isle of France. The newly-arrived missionaries expressed great concern when they learned of the Judsons' defection from the Congregationalist denomination and wrote to the board to this effect. Luther Rice, who had agreed to raise his support if appointed, revealed his own uncertainties and was baptized less than three months after arrival. Now there were three to begin the first American Baptist mission overseas.

Finding a Field

But where could the missionaries go? During the five-and-a-half months the Judsons were in India they considered a dozen fields—including Persia, Japan, and even Brazil. No way seemed to be open to them, and they had to leave India soon. They received word of the outbreak of hostilities between Britain and the United States, and authorities were particularly suspicious of U.S. citizens. Suddenly they ordered that all of the American missionaries be shipped to England. Hall and the Notts succeeded in evading police and boarding a boat for Bombay, where they were eventually able to open a mission.

The Judsons and Rice secured passage on a ship sailing for the Isle of France but were removed from it by the authorities. Finally, they obtained an official pass to board the ship, but it had already sailed. They made a wild chase overland down the coast throughout one night and the next day and managed to catch up with the ship and board it before it sailed to open sea.

Seven weeks later they landed at the Isle of France. Samuel Newell greeted them with the sad news that, due to hardships of the voyage from Calcutta, the new baby had died—as did the mother a few days later. Harriett Newell's missionary career had ended six weeks after her nineteenth birthday. Samuel Newell, broken by his loss, left to join colleagues in Bombay.

Luther Rice experienced health problems, especially with his liver, and these seemed to be aggravated by the island climate. In consultation with the Judsons he decided to return to the U.S.

temporarily to rally Baptists for mission support. He left the Isle of France in March 1813.

This island, with its isolated position and small population, seemed to offer little promise for the establishment of a mission. Most of the inhabitants were slaves, and their owners permitted no Christian work among them. The Judsons finally chose as their field the island of Penang, just off the Malayan coast. As no ships from the Isle of France were ever destined for this place, they took passage to Madras, hoping to secure transport from there to Penang before their presence could be discovered by East India Company officials. They reached Madras early in June and local authorities immediately reported their presence to Calcutta.

Judson wrote:

> It became, therefore, a moral certainty that, as soon as an order should be received at Madras, we should be again arrested and ordered to England. Our only safety appeared to consist in escaping from Madras before such an order should arrive.

He spent all available time at the wharves seeking a vessel bound for Penang—or almost anywhere! The only one leaving soon was headed for Rangoon! Friends in Madras advised against going to Burma, as had all of the others. The choice seemed simple, however: Burma or England.

The Judsons boarded the Rangoon-bound *Georgiana*. It was a Portuguese boat, old and dilapidated, obviously unseaworthy—a "crazy old vessel," as Judson called it. The only "cabin" for passengers was a tent-like cubicle of canvas on the open deck. Storms raged during the voyage. Ann was far advanced in pregnancy and quite ill and went into premature labor. The baby arrived, with no help but Adoniram's, but was dead. The boat finally arrived at Rangoon on 13 July 1813.

Rangoon had a population of perhaps 10,000. Ann, too weak to walk, was transported in an armchair with bamboo poles stuck through its sides and carriers fore and aft. The Judsons were stopped at the customs shed, where officials took a tenth of their belongings for the king. Finally they arrived at the mission house. They discovered that Felix Carey was away at Ava, the capital, on

service for the king. His wife welcomed the Judsons warmly and
shared with them a part of the spacious house.

Establishing the Burma Mission

To learn the language, the Judsons employed a teacher who knew
no English. Burmese written characters seemed rounded, the circles
varying somewhat in form and broken at various places. There
was no punctuation or spacing between words or sentences. No
printed materials or bound volumes existed in the language. "Instead of clear characters on paper," Judson wrote to Pastor Bolles,
"we find only obscure scratches on dried palm leaves strung together and called a book."

Due to disruption in communications caused by the War of
1812 and struggles with Napoleon in Europe, the Judsons did not
receive any mail from America until 5 September 1815. Due largely
to Luther Rice's energetic and widespread efforts, Baptists had
organized at a Philadelphia convention in May 1814 the General
Missionary Convention of the Baptist Denomination in the United
States of America for Foreign Missions, generally called the Triennial Convention because of its meetings once every three years.
This agency immediately appointed Judson as its missionary.

Ann gave birth to a baby boy, Roger Williams Judson, in September 1815, attended only by her husband. The baby died of
tropical fevers, however, within eight months. Both Ann and Adoniram suffered serious and extended illnesses—without the aid of
a doctor—loneliness, and discouragement.

While Ann was away in India for medical treatment, Adoniram
wrote to a friend:

> There is not an individual in the country that I can pray with, and not
> a single soul with whom I can have the least religious communion. . . .
> No Burman has, I believe, ever felt the grace of God.

The Judsons' chief concern, however, was "that Brother Rice may
not be able to join us again." They longed for missionary colleagues to help them claim Burma for Christ.

Judson, along with his full-time language studies, witnessed to his faith whenever he could, though without visible response. He wrote to Luther Rice in the U.S. that people may ask:

"What prospect of ultimate success is there?" Tell them, "As much as that there is an almighty and faithful God, who will perform his promises, and no more." If this does not satisfy them, beg them to let me stay and try it . . . and to give us our bread . . . and if we live some twenty or thirty years, they may hear from us again.

In the same letter Judson affirmed his own commitment:

If a ship was lying in the river, ready to convey me to any part of the world I should choose, and that too, with the entire approbation of all my Christian friends, I would prefer dying to embarking.

In a letter to Rice three months later Judson urged caution in the selection of missionaries:

One wrongheaded, obstinate fellow would ruin us. Humble, quiet, persevering men; men of sound, sterling talents (though perhaps, not brilliant), of decent accomplishments, and some natural aptitude to acquire a language; men of amiable, yielding temper, willing to take the lowest place, to be the least of all and the servants of all; men who enjoy much closet religion, who live near to God, and are willing to suffer anything for Christ's sake, without being proud of it. . . . But oh, how unlike to this description is the writer of it.

The first missionary recruit was the printer George Hough, who arrived with his family in October 1816. He spent several months at the Serampore print shop enroute. Carey and his colleagues presented him with a printing press, Burmese types, and other equipment to take to Rangoon.

The Judsons and the Houghs drew up "articles of agreement" expressing their sole purpose "to introduce the religion of Jesus Christ into the empire of Burma" through "translating, printing, and distributing the Holy Scriptures, preaching the gospel, circulating religious tracts, and promoting the instruction of native children." In a letter accompanying the articles, Judson wrote to the foreign mission secretary: "We are now united, both as a church of Christ and as a mission society. . . . We consider the mission established in this land."

In addition to the Burmese language, Judson made a thorough study of Pali. An offshoot of Sanscrit, this language had been brought to Burma with the Buddhist religion centuries before. It furnished the words and thought patterns for religious concepts. To translate the Bible and do Christian writing, Pali—although long a dead language—seemed indispensable to one as thorough as Judson in his work. He prepared a grammar and dictionary of the Pali language.

He also wrote two tracts in Burmese, one a summary of the Christian faith and the other—written in collaboration with Ann—a catechism for children. Hough printed these tracts soon after he arrived. Judson then completed the translation of the Gospel of Matthew and published it. This was apparently the first printing ever done in Burma.

Converts Despite Threats

While Judson was out of the country, Hough received a menacing order to appear at the courthouse in Rangoon. There, petty officials harassed him and threatened expulsion from Burma. Ann went with him later to the viceroy, who reprimanded the subordinates who had made the threats. Hough was unnerved by this experience, however, and decided he could do his printing work better in Calcutta. He left soon afterward, taking his family and the mission press with him.

Additional recruits arrived from America: the Edward Wheelocks and James Colmans. Both men had bad health, and Wheelock died within a year.

Judson, always on the lookout for ways to make the gospel known among the Burmese, decided to build a *zayat*. Quite familiar and traditional in Burma, this was a roadside hut or larger enclosure where travelers could rest and talk, or hear a lecture. Buddhist teachers often used *zayats* as places of instruction for the people. Judson built his *zayat* on Pagoda Road, perhaps the most heavily-traveled artery of the Rangoon area. The *zayat* measured twenty-seven feet by eighteen feet and cost about $200. The back of its lot adjoined mission-house property. The front third of the structure was a porch, built of bamboo and thatch and open toward the road. The main room, of whitewashed boards, had four doors and four windows. In a small back room, Ann had meetings with women or children.

The *zayat* opened in April 1819. Judson held regular worship services there. Fifteen persons, besides children, attended the first service. At other times he would sit on the porch, calling out in Burmese to passersby, "Ho, every one that thirsteth, come to the waters." Burmese were accustomed to such methods, and many stopped to speak with him. He explained the Christian faith, answered questions, and placed printed material into the hands of those who seemed to be interested—if they could read.

After attending services at the *zayat* for a while and holding long discussions with Judson, a Burmese by the name of Maung Nau (Maung, or Moung as Judson and others wrote it at the time, was the title for a young man) became an inquirer. In his journal, the missionary described him as "thirty-five years old, no family, middling abilities, quite poor."

Following the service on 9 May, Maung Nau publicly declared himself a disciple of Christ's. Judson warned him that he had "nothing to expect in this world but persecution, and perhaps death," but he declared his determination to be faithful to Christ even if no Burmese would ever join him. Judson baptized this first convert in a nearby pond on 27 June 1819, six years after the arrival of Adoniram and Ann in Burma.

Four months later, two more converts were baptized. Others made professions of faith but withdrew when state authorities ordered an investigation. This new indication of official disapproval caused a sharp fall in attendance at the *zayat*. "I sometimes sat there whole days without a single visitor," Adoniram reported," though it is the finest part of the year, and many are constantly passing." He received unreasonable tax assessments, threats, and annoyances from the authorities.

Trampled by the Golden Feet

Judson decided on a bold step to determine whether his work, and the change of religion by Burmese would be tolerated in Burma. He would go to the new king, a more intolerant Buddhist than his predecessor. The new "emperor" began his reign with the torture and execution of numerous members of his family who might conceivably challenge his sovereignty. Many thousands of others were reportedly put to death.

Judson and Colman set out for Ava toward the end of December. They traveled up the Irrawady River in a boat six feet wide in the middle and forty feet long. With them were ten rowmen, a steersman, a washwoman, two cooks, a head man, and an English adventurer desirous of service under the Burmese king. The Englishman was the gunner, responsible for protecting the party against robbers who worked along the riverbank.

The 350-mile trip took just over a month. In Ava, through an official he had known in Rangoon, Judson secured an audience with the king for the day following his arrival. The Americans would be permitted to approach the Golden Feet! (Everything about the king was called golden.) The missionaries returned after making the arrangements to sleep in the boat, but it was a sleepless night. "Tomorrow's dawn will usher in the most eventful day of our lives," Judson wrote in his journal. "Tomorrow's eve will close on the bloom or the blight of our fondest hopes."

Even the slightest business with a public official required a suitable gift, and deciding what to give the king presented a problem. The missionaries had settled on a six-volume English Bible covered with gold leaf.

Eventually Judson and Colman were ushered into a great upper hall whose entire surface was covered with gold leaf. The Golden Foot was approaching, a counselor informed them. As the king strode majestically forward, clothed in rich attire and bearing a gold-sheathed sword, all others in the room knelt and pressed their foreheads against the floor obsequiously. Judson and Colman knelt but with heads erect. This attracted the king's attention. "Who are these?" he asked.

"The teachers, great king," said Judson.

"What, you speak Burman—the priests that I heard of last night?" the king inquired.

Judson answered this question and others about the time of arrival, whether they were like the Portuguese priests, why they dressed as they did, and whether they were married. Then his majesty sat down on an elevated seat and listened to the reading of a petition the missionaries had prepared. It requested

> that royal permission be given, that we, taking refuge in the royal power, may preach our religion in these dominions, and that those who are pleased with our preaching, and wish to listen to and be guided by it, whether foreigners or Burmans, may be exempt from government molestation.

The king took the petition and read it through himself then returned it to the counselor without a word. He also threw to the floor a beautifully bound tract Judson had prepared and given to him. One of the king's ministers opened a volume of the gift Bible the missionaries had brought, but his majesty took no notice.

The chief counselor expressed his royal master's will:

> Why do you ask for such permission? Have not the Portuguese, the English, the Mussulmans, and people of all other religions full liberty to practice and worship according to their own customs? In regard to the objects of your petition, his majesty gives no order. In regard to your sacred books, his majesty has no use for them: take them away.

All hopes of the missionaries for official toleration crashed to the ground. They remained a week or so in Ava, making official contacts through two Englishmen who resided there. When one of these approached the emperor in their behalf his majesty laughed and said,

> What, they have come presuming to convert us to their religion? Let them leave our capital. We have no desire to receive their instruction. Perhaps they may find some of their countrymen in Rangoon who may be willing to listen to them.

Sadly, the mission party returned to Rangoon. On the downriver trip Judson and Colman discussed what course they should take in regard to the mission. They decided it would be best to move it across the border into Chittagong, where the British were in a control but the people spoke a dialect of Burmese. A few converts remained in Chittagong from an earlier mission out of Serampore.

The missionaries wondered what effect their failure at Ava would have on converts in Rangoon. "We thought that, if one out of the three remained firm, it was as much as we could reasonably hope for," Judson wrote in his diary. The new believers were of course troubled on hearing the discouraging report, but they did not waver. Judson wrote, "They all, to a man, appeared immovably the same; yea, rather advanced in zeal and energy."

The saddest part for the converts was the intention of the missionaries to leave them. One of them said,

Notwithstanding present difficulties and dangers, it is to be remembered that this work is not yours or ours, but the work of God. If he give light, the religion will spread. Nothing can impede it.

Another suggested that the missionaries remain until there should be "a little church of ten, with a teacher set over them."

This unexpected fervor and faithfulness moved the missionaries deeply. They reconsidered their plan. In order to take advantage of the opportunity in populous Chittagong, it was decided the Colmans should go there and the Judsons would remain in Rangoon as long as residence and work were possible. If the position became untenable, they might still be able to take refuge in Chittagong, perhaps taking Burmese converts with them. Colman labored faithfully in Chittagong until his death two years later.

It seemed inadvisable to conduct public services in Rangoon and to call passersby into the *zayat*. Meetings took place, with small attendance, behind closed doors. Several more converts were baptized. One of these, a prominent man, was denounced to the authorities. Obliged to flee for his life, he took tracts with him and continued his witness in the interior of the country. The tenth convert was the first woman to be baptized. None of this activity was generally known. Most people assumed Judson worked only among foreigners.

Brighter Hopes for Royal Tolerance

Ann Judson's health failed, due primarily to liver disease. A voyage to Calcutta failed to bring lasting relief. Adoniram sadly recognized the necessity for her to return to America for treatment. "I feel as if I was on the scaffold, and signing, as it were, my own death warrant," he wrote to Hough in Calcutta, which would be her first stop. "However, two years will pass away at last," he added—hoping she would be back by then and restored to health.

Ann stopped for a time in England and Scotland, speaking in churches as much as her physical condition permitted. At the urging of an English publisher, she prepared for the press a book that was published in England and America. The U.S. edition was entitled, *A Particular Relation of the American Baptist Mission to the Burman Empire*. Ann spent nine months in America. Somewhat restored in health, she sailed on 22 June for Calcutta, accompanied by the Jonathan Wades—new appointees for the Burma mission.

Other new missionaries had come to Burma while Ann was gone. Dr. Jonathan Price, whose wife died soon after their arrival, gained a great reputation for his surgical skill, especially in removal of eye cataracts. He was the only qualified physician in Burma, and reports of his work soon reached the king. His majesty summoned Price to the capital. Judson accompanied him, in order to take advantage of any openings for planting the Gospel more securely. (The church in Rangoon then had eighteen members.)

Judson and Price left for Ava 28 August 1822 in a boat provided by the government. Upon arrival, they were received in audience by the king several times. His majesty manifested interest primarily in the medical knowledge of Dr. Price, but on about the third visit he took notice of Judson.

"And you, in black, what are you? A medical man too?"

"Not a medical man," Judson replied, "but a teacher of religion."

After several questions about this religion, the king asked the alarming one—whether any had embraced it.

"Not here," answered the missionary evasively.

"Are there any in Rangoon?" persisted the monarch.

"There are a few," Judson admitted.

"Are they foreigners?"

Judson trembled inwardly at this question, realizing that a truthful reply might involve the little church in ruin. He knew he must give an honest answer and leave the consequences to God. "There are some foreigners," he said, "and some Burmans."

The king remained silent for a few tense moments, then he changed the subject, asking in a friendly way numerous questions about religion, geography, and astronomy. He later authorized Judson to invite American ships to Burma, assuring them protection and offering every facility for trade.

Some weeks later his majesty raised again the question of Burmese who had embraced Christianity. "Are they real Burmans?" he inquired. "Do they dress like other Burmans?" Judson answered these and other questions, mentioning that he preached in Burmese every Sunday. This impressed the king and he said, "Let us hear how you preach."

Judson hesitated, then was ordered by one of the king's ministers to proceed. He began in a simple and reverent way, ascribing glory to God, setting forth the perfections of God and the "law" of the Christian gospel. His majesty interrupted and asked some questions, including one regarding Christianity's attitude toward Gautama the Buddha. Adoniram replied, "We regard him as a wise man and a great teacher but do not call him God." After a few more questions, the king retired from the room. He made it clear, however, that he desired Price and Judson to remain in Ava.

This invitation they welcomed, hoping they might be able to win some high officials to Christ. The sister and half brother of the king had indicated interest. In any case it seemed highly advisable to establish a Christian mission in Ava. The king intervened personally to secure property for the Americans. Judson had a small caretaker's shelter erected on the lot made available to him, and he returned to Rangoon. The king consented to his leaving when Judson promised to come back to Ava with his belongings when his wife returned from America. Price remained in Ava.

Upon arrival in Rangoon, Adoniram learned that Ann would not be returning for several months at least. He plunged with abandon into his translation work, to which he had given as much time as possible through the years. By the middle of July he had completed translation of the New Testament, along with a summary of the Old Testament in twelve chapters.

Ann returned early in December 1823, accompanied by the Jonathan Wades. Adoniram did not want to delay the move to Ava any longer, and when Ann arrived he had a boat ready to take them upriver. "My baggage was immediately taken from the ship to the boat," she wrote in a letter home, "and in seven days from my arrival, we were on our way to the capital."

There had long been rumors of war between Burma and British forces in India. The Burmese were determined to take over a province that bordered on Bengal India and was under British rule. On their trip upriver the Judsons saw encampments of Burmese troops said to number 30,000. They were obviously on their way to attack the British.

After arrival in the capital city, Judson had a house built on the property secured the previous year, and it was ready in two weeks. He called several times at the king's court, but the atmosphere seemed entirely different from what it had been before. Foreigners were out of favor, to say the least. Friendly ministers of state had been replaced by those who had no sympathy for the British or any other foreigners.

Still, Judson tried to start his work immediately with a full mission program. He hoped the authorities would see that the Americans were in no way connected with political and military affairs. He began daily worship services at the little mission house. On Sundays he conducted services in Dr. Price's house in the village of Sagaing across the river.

Ann started a class for girls, with three enrolled, teaching practical skills such as sewing as well as reading and writing. Two of the little girls were sisters; their mother had become deranged, and the father turned them over to the Judsons to educate. Ann gave them the names of her sisters, Abby and Mary. Despite the war clouds, the Judsons felt optimistic and considered the outlook rather bright. It was the calm before the storm.

Missionaries in Chains

The Burmese king declared war against the British. He had no doubt of an early victory and the capture of British territory for Burma. On 24 May, however, the shattering news reached the capital that the British had occupied Rangoon.

Sixteen days later as the Judsons were preparing for the noon meal, an official burst into their home, accompanied by a large number of assistants. Among them was a "Spotted Face," known by his markings as a former criminal, now a "son of the prison"— jailor and executioner. He had a spot tattooed on each cheek. His presence was a bad sign. "You are called by the king," said the official. This was the form of speech customarily used in making an arrest.

The spotted man instantly seized Judson and threw him to the floor, tying his arms together at his back with a special type of cord that the Burmese used for torture. He was dragged from the house. Ann turned to their faithful servant Maung Ing, an early convert, and told him to follow them. This he did and saw Judson taken to that well-known place of horrors, the so-called Death Prison. Maung Ing returned to Mrs. Judson with these fearful tidings.

Inside the prison walls, Judson was turned over to the chief Spotted Face, a heartless sadist who made the prisoners call him Father. One could see by the brands on his chest that he had himself been consigned to prison for murder. Now he was in charge of all the other prisoners.

Judson was taken to a stone block in the center of the yard where three pairs of heavy iron fetters were fastened to his ankles, then he was thrown into the common room of the prison. About thirty by forty feet in size, this room was already crowded with approximately fifty miserable prisoners, including some women. Judson recognized three Britishers, one of whom was Henry Gouger, a wealthy trader still in his twenties with whom the Judsons had developed a cordial friendship. He had cashed their letters of credit from Calcutta, thus providing the mission with funds. Later in the day Price was brought into the prison, then an elderly Greek merchant and a young Armenian.

In the evening the jailers stuck a long bamboo pole between the fettered legs of each prisoner, then elevated it until only the shoulders and head of the prisoners rested on the ground. In this uncomfortable position they were forced to pass the long hours of each night. The jailers considered the precaution necessary, since the frail board walls would not prevent escape by desperate prisoners.

After Adoniram had been dragged from home, Ann destroyed all of their journals and letters. Among these materials were correspondence with Britishers and minute descriptions of Burmese life that might arouse suspicions. Before she completed the job, she heard a police official at the door yelling for her to come outside. She did so and was questioned at length. The official ordered gates of the mission yard to be shut; no one was to go in or out. A gang of ruffians was left on guard. With her little Burmese girls, Ann retired for a sleepless night.

After several days of ingenious efforts to send messages, involving generous bribery of the chief guard, Ann got word to the city governor asking for a permit to visit him with a present. This stratagem finally succeeded. The governor received her politely, and she pled for release of the Americans. He said it was not in his power to release them from prison or irons, but he could make their situation more comfortable. He sent Ann to his head officer, who demanded coins worth $100 at the time and other gifts. After payment had been made, the governor signed orders allowing her to enter the prison and do what she could.

At the prison Ann was allowed only the briefest contact with her husband, but finally—after the payment of many more bribes —he was taken from the common room and put under an open shed in the prison yard. The other foreigners, making about the same payment that Ann had, were likewise removed to the shed. For a time after that Ann was not allowed in the prison yard, but she sent food and sleeping mats.

When she was allowed to speak again with Adoniram, Ann asked what she should do about his New Testament translation manuscript. She had temporarily buried it with some other things under the mission house. He told her to sew it into a pillow so hard the jailers would not take it from him for their own use, which she did.

Through royal relatives with whom Ann had previous contacts and judicious placing of gifts and bribes, she got a petition through to the queen. The latter replied, "The teachers will not die. Let them remain as they are."

The king's men were confiscating foreigners' property. At Gouger's place they took gold, silver, and other items valued then at $50,000. On their way back to the palace with this loot they politely informed Mrs. Judson that they would visit her house the next day. This warning gave her time to hide some small items and considerable sums in silver under the house. She knew the danger involved in this action but also knew she would be unable to live and help Adoniram without resources to turn into cash.

The confiscation party, numbering about fifty men, came as promised the next day. They took most things of value, including some money Ann had left to be found, but at her request they made only a list of clothing and other personal effects rather than taking everything.

Ann continued to press every contact in the royal household and in the process won many friends, as she always seemed to do in any situation. None, however, dared present a request to the king for the prisoners. With the British pushing ever closer toward the capital, it was considered almost suicidal for anyone to ask favors for Englishmen and other foreigners.

Brave, unprotected Ann never gave up. She later wrote to Adoniram's brother:

> For the seven following months, hardly a day passed that I did not visit some one of the members of government or branches of the royal family in order to gain their influence in our behalf. My prevailing opinion was that my husband would suffer a violent death, and that I should, of course, become a slave and languish out a miserable though short existence in the tyrannic hands of some unfeeling monster.

The Death March

Ann provided all of Adoniram's food, and the other foreigners were supplied by their servants. Those prisoners who had no one to send them food died of starvation, as none was furnished by the authorities. Ann usually brought the food herself rather than sending it by a servant, so that she could be with Adoniram for a few minutes each time.

During the periods when Ann was not allowed to visit Adoniram at all, they communicated in secret. At first they did this through messages written on a hard flat pancake placed under the rice. He would write his reply on a wet tile, the writing becoming visible only when the tile had dried. Then they devised the more convenient method of writing on a small piece of paper that was rolled tightly and inserted in the spout of the teapot sent with the food.

The fare was usually very drab—only rice and fish. One day, however, Ann worked hard to find suitable substitute ingredients to prepare a mince pie. As she was not permitted to go to the prison that day, she sent the meal by Maung Ing. When Adoniram uncovered the lunch and saw what his beloved wife had done, his emotions overcame him. Was it not enough, he later said in describing his emotions, that she had borne the brunt of their humiliation, taunts and insults, the dangers and toils of trying to save his life and reduce his sufferings? This action was too much. He dropped his head on his knees and tears flowed down on the iron fetters. He could not eat. He thrust the precious meal into the hands of Price and hurried, as best he could with heavily shackled feet, out into the corner of the yard and wept without restraint.

Meanwhile, Burmese forces continued to meet defeat in every battle. Their main army—60,000 strong—was virtually destroyed as a fighting force by an army of 1,300 British and 2,500 Sepoys from India.

Suddenly, on 1 March, foreigners in the prison were taken into the yard, shackled with two extra fetters then thrust back into the common room. Rumor had it that they were to be executed at 3 A.M. Spotted Faces were all sharpening their huge knives. Judson led the prisoners in prayer, then several other foreigners prayed. Execution did not take place the next morning, but prisoners were kept in the common room.

Ann redoubled her efforts. She went to her friend the governor, who was over the prison administration. "When I am ordered to execute them," he told her, "the least I can do is to put them out of sight." Three times, he said, the queen's brother had ordered him to execute the white prisoners, but he promised "Mrs. Judson" as he had before that he would never put her husband to death.

After a month in the inner prison Judson had high fever and was critically ill. It seemed he would surely die if obliged to remain in the filthy and vermin-infested place, crowded in with so many others. Ann wore the old governor down with her incessant entreaties. He finally allowed her to build a little bamboo hut for her husband in the prison yard, and there his health improved. He had the "New Testament pillow" in his possession, having given the Spotted Face who took it a better one in exchange.

To save the time required for the two-mile walk from the Judson home, Ann secured permission to build for herself a bamboo hut on part of the governor's property, just across the road from the prison.

One day as she was with Adoniram, after he had been in prison for eleven months, a messenger came with word that she should go at once to the governor's house. Ann promised Adoniram she would return to inform him of the results of the meeting.

Just after she left, one of the Spotted Faces rushed in to where Judson was and yanked him out into the yard. He snatched off the prisoner's hat and shoes, took his bedding, removed the chains, tied a rope around his waist, and hustled him away to the courthouse where the other foreign prisoners were already assembled. They were then tied two and two and under heavy guard marched off toward Amarapura, which was about four miles away.

The time was near midday, in the hottest season of the year. Judson's feet blistered, and soon there seemed to be no skin left on the soles. Other foreign prisoners had discarded shoes at the beginning in Death Prison, so their feet were somewhat toughened.

Judson had continued to wear his shoes, but this morning they had been taken from him. He was still feverish from his illness and had eaten no breakfast. Almost in delirium from pain, he felt the temptation to end it all by throwing himself over the side of a high bridge the prisoners crossed, but then he realized this would be a heinous sin.

Gouger's servant—walking beside this horrible procession—helped as he could by taking off his headdress, tearing the strip of cloth into parts, then giving half to his master and half to Judson. They wrapped the cloth around their feet as best they could as they walked, for no one was allowed to stop even for a minute. Those who fell behind received a cruel beating. A corpulent Greek prisoner could not keep up and was beaten to death by the guards.

The Heroine of Oung-pen-la

The miserable prisoners were kept in Amarapoora that night. The next day they were loaded onto carts—hardly any of them able to walk—and taken to Oung-pen-la, a village four miles farther. There, still tied two and two, they were dumped into the yard of a tumbledown, unoccupied prison.

Soon afterward a cart pulled into the prison yard. In it were Ann, her baby daughter Maria (who was born in January 1825), the two Burmese girls who lived with the Judsons, and their Bengali cook.

"'Why have you come?" wailed Adoniram. "I hoped you would not follow, for you cannot live here." The outlook was certainly bleak. Ann had counted on buying food at a local market, but there was no market. The head jailor finally agreed to let her use a small storeroom attached to his own house. There she fell on the filthy floor to sleep, beside her baby and the two girls.

At nightfall the prisoners were brought into the common room and their shackled feet raised high by a bamboo pole as in the Death Prison. The mosquitos swarming from the rice fields lighted on their lacerated feet and caused maddening pain. Then the jailor mercifully lowered the pole enough for the prisoners to fan insects away.

The next morning, Ann told Adoniram of her experiences during the previous two days when she went to the governor's house in response to his urgent call. His excellency desired to speak only about his new watch and other inconsequential matters. He was unusually talkative and held her for a long time. As Ann left the governor's house, she met a servant who was running toward her with the unhappy news that all the white prisoners had been taken away.

Ann ran up and down the streets asking everyone she met if they had seen the prisoners, without obtaining any helpful information. She then raced back to the governor and learned from him that they were being taken toward Amarapoora, for what purpose he did not know. He admitted having summoned her from Death Prison so that she would not be there while the dirty work was going on. "You can do nothing more for your husband," he said with deep emotion. "Take care of yourself."

Not one to care for herself when her Adoniram was in mortal danger, Ann gathered some things together. She took the children and the Bengali cook—whom Ann had brought from Bengal in India on her return from America in 1823—and set off in a boat down the Nootangi River toward Amarapoora. There she learned that the prisoners had left two hours before for Oung-pen-la. They made the rest of the journey over very rough roads in a springless cart.

The storeroom of the jailor's house served as Ann's home for "six months of wretchedness," as she later described it. There was no furniture, not even a table or seat of any kind. As usual, however, the courageous woman made the best of her difficult situation and gave herself fully in trying to help the others.

The day after their arrival, Mary—who, although only eight years-old, had been Ann's helper with the baby—broke out with smallpox. Ann had to tend her all the time she could spare from Adoniram, whose mangled feet still tortured him and brought on high fever. She had no medicines and could get no help in the area. Finding food was a problem. She had to carry the baby constantly as she went from one to another of the patients.

Ann inoculated Maria from another child that had smallpox, then from Mary she inoculated Abby and the jailor's children. Maria's injection did not take. She contracted the disease and suffered with it for three months, but the other children escaped with the mild effects of successful inoculation. Ann's fame spread throughout the area and children were brought from far and near for her to inoculate.

Conditions at this place were somewhat better than in Death Prison. An open shed was prepared for the use of prisoners by day, and they were returned to the common room at night. They were chained two and two at first, but—as the jailers had an insufficient supply of chains—this practice was discontinued. Each prisoner had only one pair of fetters. Judson's health began to improve, but he was unable to stand on his injured feet for six weeks after arrival at Oung-pen-la.

One night the prisoners heard the roars of a lion and realized the caged beast was being placed in the prison yard. Not even the head jailer understood why it had been sent there. Actually the king had received the lion as a gift from a foreigner about a year before the beginning of the war and felt fond of the noble beast. As the Burmese began to suffer humiliating defeats, superstitious courtiers suggested that since the British bore a lion on their standard, this lion must be a demonic ally of the British.

The king, desiring to keep the lion, denied that there was any connection between it and the British victories. He finally agreed that it be placed in the Oung-pen-la prison yard but expressly stipulated that it not be killed without his order. The queen's brother, meanwhile, gave secret directions that the lion should be given no food. The fearful sight and sound of the starving beast, as it writhed in hunger pains day after day and night after night, was hard on the prisoners. They had seen men starved, but still they were not prepared for this.

When the poor animal finally died it was pulled out and buried, but the cage remained. Judson secured permission to occupy the cage himself, and from that time the jailor locked him up in it each night. This was much cleaner and more healthful than sleeping in the common room with feet raised high on a bamboo pole.

The Victims Used by the Burmese

With inadequate food, miserable living quarters, and endless labors for the sick, it is not surprising that Ann's health deteriorated. She had a light case of smallpox then later an oriental disease that usually proved fatal to foreigners. Her old liver problem returned. Already so weak she could hardly stand, she set off in a cart for

Ava to get some of the medicines which she had left at the governor's house.

While in Ava she had such a severe attack that she lost hope of recovery but dosed herself with laudanum so as to be able to get back to Oung-pen-la and die near the prison. Driven by her indomitable willpower, she made it back but arrived in such a state that the Bengali cook broke into tears when he saw her. She crawled onto her mat in the room at the jailor's house, and there she had to remain almost all the time for more than two months. Ann never recovered entirely from the effects of this severe illness.

The faithful cook cared for both Judsons, although they could no longer pay his wages. Ann wrote to Adoniram's brother:

> I have frequently known him not to taste of food till near night, in consequence of having to go so far for food and water, and in order to have Mr. Judson's dinner ready at the usual hour. He never complained, never asked for his wages, and never for a moment hesitated to go anywhere, or to perform any act we required.

Gouger's servant continued to be loyal too, bringing food regularly from Ava.

Little Maria suffered greatly during this period. Ann's illness deprived her of usual nourishment, and neither a nurse nor a drop of milk could be obtained in the village. Ann gave presents to the chief jailers and thereby obtained permission for Adoniram to leave the prison—still wearing his chains—and go from house to house in the village with the emaciated Maria in his arms, begging a bit of milk from nursing mothers. Thus the infant's life was saved, but often she went hungry. "Her cries in the night," Ann said, "were heartrending."

As Burmese forces continued to lose ground to the British, the king tried one after another of his generals as commander-in-chief. Each one seemed confident that he could drive the British out of Burma. The prisoners learned later that it had been on order from the most cruel of these generals that they had been brought to Oung-pen-la. This was the general's native district, and he intended to launch his new offensive against the British from there. As part of the celebration he had proposed that the foreign prisoners be buried alive before him. While preparations were being made, however, this general himself came under suspicion of high treason and was executed without trial.

Finally, the hopelessness of the Burmese cause became evident even to the Burmese king. He desired to treaty for peace, and for this he needed the services of Judson as interpreter. When Judson was taken from the Oung-pen-la prison for this purpose, the jailers refused to allow Ann to leave with him until they received substantial bribes.

Judson was placed again in prison when they reached Ava, although not the Death Prison. The next day, he was taken by boat down the river to a Burmese camp. The little boat provided no protection from the elements and was so crowded that no one could lie down. By the time of arrival at camp three days later, Judson had a violent fever. Still the Burmese made him work at translation, and his condition became worse. He was kept at this place for six weeks, and at times fever drove him into delirium.

Ann remained in Ava, and in her weakened condition she was seized by the dreaded spotted fever (cerebral spinal meningitis). She felt sure she would not recover. Soon she was losing consciousness, sometimes for days at a time. Price was released from prison about this time and could give some medical assistance, but there seemed little hope. "She is dead," said a Burmese neighbor who came in to see her, "and if the king of angels should come in, he could not recover her."

Judson was returned to Ava and confined there temporarily. Officials intended to send him back to Oung-pen-la. Ann learned that he was in Ava and dispatched Maung Ing to find him. Adoniram then sent this dependable helper to the governor. The good old man personally stood security for the missionary and ordered his release. Judson rushed home, but he had not been told of the serious illness of his beloved wife. The sight of her wasted form, spent for him, almost broke his heart. She had begun to regain some strength, but the process was slow and never to be complete.

Judson and Price were used for further official negotiations with the British commander, Sir Archibald Campbell. Meanwhile, the Burmese made a last desperate military effort, even while they sued for peace; this of course proved to be totally futile. Sir Archibald refused to discuss peace unless the foreigners, including the

American missionaries, were released with all their possessions. By this time Ann felt able to travel, so she and Adoniram left for the British camp at Yantabo.

A Pleasant Interlude

Years later, as Adoniram Judson listened to several persons discussing what the greatest worldly pleasures had been, he and Ann related some happy experiences.

Judson said with an expression of impatience:

> These men are not qualified to judge. I know of a much higher pleasure than that. What do you think of floating down the Irrawaddy on a cool, moonlight evening with your wife by your side and your baby in your arms, free—all free? But you cannot understand it, either; it needs a twenty-one months' qualification; and I can never regret my twenty-one months of misery when I recall that one delicious thrill. I think I have had a better appreciation of what heaven may be, ever since.

Upon reaching the port of the British camp, Adoniram proceeded at once to Sir Archibald's headquarters, but Ann remained on the boat to rest overnight. The next morning the general sent his own son with other officers to escort her from the boat to the place prepared for the Judsons. He had provided for them a tent, larger and better fitted out than his own; it even had a veranda. The Judsons were his honored guests at meals. Ann related later that he

> treated us with the kindness of a father rather than as strangers of another country. . . . I presume to say that no persons on earth were ever happier than we were during the fortnight we passed at the English camp.

A few days after their arrival the general was to receive a group of Burmese commissioners. He decided to make it a festive occasion in honor of the Judsons. Gold and crimson streamers were everywhere and banners on the tents.

Adoniram later recalled the event:

> When the dinner hour arrived, the company marched in couples to the music of the band toward the table, led by the general, who walked along. As they came opposite the tent with the veranda before it,

suddenly the music ceased. The whole procession stood still, and—while the wondering Burmese turned their eager eyes in every direction, doubtful as to what would be the next act in the little drama, so curious to them as strangers—the general entered the tent.

In a moment he reappeared with the lady on his arm—no stranger to the conscious commissioners—whom he led to the table and seated at his own right hand. The abashed commissioners slid into their seats shrinkingly, where they sat as though transfixed by a mixture of astonishment and fear.

"I fancy these gentlemen must be old acquaintances of yours, Mrs. Judson," General Campbell remarked, amused by what he began to suspect, though he did not fully understand it; "and judging from their appearance you must have treated them very ill."

Mrs. Judson smiled. "I do not know," she answered—fixing her eyes on the most disturbed one and with perhaps a mischievous enjoyment of his anxiety—"unless his memory may be too busy. He is an old acquaintance of mine, and may probably infer danger to himself from seeing me under your protection."

Ann then related how that when her husband was critically ill with fever in the Death Prison at Ava, with five pairs of fetters about his ankles, she walked several miles to this man's house to ask a favor. He kept her waiting for hours and then gave a curt refusal to her request. As she turned sadly away, he noticed with covetous eyes the silk umbrella she carried and snatched it away from her.

Ann tried to explain that it would be dangerous for her to walk the long way home under the hot noonday sun, without protection. She begged the man that if he must take her umbrella to at least give her a paper one to protect her from the scorching rays.

In relating the story, Judson said:

He laughed and, turning the very suffering that had wasted her into a jest, said only stout people were in danger of a sunstroke—the sun could not find such as she, so turned her from the door.

The British officers cast withering glances at the accused commissioner. This man, although unable to understand what had been said, knew the gist of it well enough. Perspiration oozed from his face, which was distorted with fear. The other Burmese commissioners were obviously uncomfortable also. All but one of them had personally treated her with indignity on one or more occasions while her husband was imprisoned.

"I never thought I was over and above vindictive," Judson said in his account of the event, "but really it was one of the richest scenes I ever beheld."

The Letter with a Black Seal

After two pleasant weeks in the British camp, the Judsons prepared to return to Rangoon. General Campbell provided his own gunboat to take them. They faced the task of attempting to gather the remnant of the little church and reorganize the work of the mission.

In conversations with the Burmese authorities, however, Judson understood that the king was still unwilling to grant religious tolerance to his subjects. It seemed advisable, therefore, to establish headquarters of the mission somewhere in territory that was being annexed by the British. The Judsons chose Amherst, a new settlement designed as the future capital of the ceded provinces, and moved there at the beginning of July 1826.

Civil commissioner John Crawford asked Judson, who knew the language and the people so well, to accompany him to Ava for the negotiation of a commercial treaty. Judson felt unwilling to do this. He opposed in principle the missionaries' spending time in secular enterprises and was eager to reestablish the mission. Ann encouraged him to render the service, however, and Crawford won him by promising to try to get a clause guaranteeing religious liberty inserted into the commercial treaty.

Having settled Ann and little Maria comfortably in Amherst, Adoniram set out with the British commissioners for Ava. The consultations began at the end of September. The king delayed and complicated the negotiations as much as possible and clearly stated that the agreement would contain no toleration clause.

While in Ava, Adoniram received several letters from Ann telling about the opening of a mission school in Amherst, with Maung

Ing as teacher, and the completion of a mission house into which she moved on 14 September. Nothing in her letters caused concern except the declining health of little Maria. On 18 October the British superintendent of Amherst wrote to Judson that the missionary's wife had suffered an attack of fever but was much better.

The next letter from Amherst reached Judson on 24 November; it had a black seal. The man who brought it said, "I am sorry to have to inform you of the death of your child." The letter was from the assistant superintendent of Amherst.

Adoniram opened the letter in his room, thankful at least that Ann had been spared. He had prepared himself for the worst in regard to Maria, for she was very ill. He broke the black seal and began to read, expecting to learn the details of little Maria's passing. In a few seconds it dawned on him with horror that the letter was not about the child at all, but his dear Ann. The messenger had been mistaken, or was perhaps trying to prepare him for the shock.

The letter began,

> My dear Sir, to one who has suffered so much and with such exemplary fortitude, there needs but little preface to tell a tale of distress. It were cruel indeed to torture you with doubt and suspense. To sum up the unhappy tidings in a few words, Mrs. Judson is no more.

The dreadful words hit poor Adoniram as a stunning blow, and with extreme difficulty he read the rest of the letter. Early in October Ann had been attacked by a violent fever. At intervals it abated, but she felt from the first that she would not recover. A British doctor attended her faithfully, but she finally expired on 24 October, exactly a month before Adoniram received the letter. She was buried under a hopia tree near the spot where the Judsons first set foot in Amherst.

The work of the commission in Ava finally came to an end, and Judson reached Amherst on 24 January 1827. His little daughter was cared for by the Wades, who had returned to Burma after spending the war years in Bengal, India. Maria did not know her father and turned in alarm from him. He went to the grave under the hopia tree to shed his tears. Maria's health declined again, and she died in April—six months after the death of her mother. She too was buried under the hopia tree.

Adoniram attempted to give himself to the work regardless of his grief. Though the strain eventually proved too great for him personally, meanwhile the mission activities continued. Judson and the other missionariee moved to Moulmein, the new capital about twenty-five miles upriver, which already had a population of about 15,000. This became the central station of the Baptist mission.

The Battle for Holiness

Burmese workers were sent from the Moulmein mission center, and additional stations were established in the ceded territories of the Chittagong area in the northwest and the Tenasarim promontory to the southeast. Judson wrote to the mission board requesting recruits to staff the new stations. These areas were as much a part of Burma, the missionaries felt, as those ruled by the "emperor." Judson wrote the board, "It is to be hoped that the influence of the gospel preached here will ultimately be felt throughout the whole country."

In Moulmein the missionaries set up a full program of work. They held public services of worship on Sundays, for which attendance soon increased to about seventy, and devotional meetings each evening. Wade spent his days in a mission *zayat* in a prominent location; Judson had his *zayat* in another part of the town. George Boardman, a new missionary, conducted a boys' school, and his wife assisted Mrs. Wade at a girls' school.

Judson began work again on Bible translation. The pillow containing the New Testament manuscript, taken from him with other personal effects on the day the foreigners were removed from Death Prison, was thrown away as worthless after its cover had been removed. Maung Ing searched around the prison a few hours later, saw the pillow, and took it home as a keepsake of his beloved teacher. Months later he discovered the manuscript inside and delivered it to the grateful missionary. Judson went through the entire work and made many improvements, then had it printed. He also started work again on the Old Testament translation.

He was very thorough in all his translation and worked directly from the original languages, using every scholarly aid available. Judson saturated himself in Burmese literature to capture every shade of meaning for the words, keeping Burmese assistants constantly at his side and discussing doubtful points with many experts. He usually completed twenty-five or thirty verses in a full day's work of translation. In spite of exhausting his powers in the work, Judson felt distressed to find that grief at the loss of his beloved wife and other sorrows remained in full force. His father's death had come soon after Ann's, as had Maria's.

Searching his soul for basic reasons to explain his depression, Judson concluded that he was a miserably selfish creature. How else could one explain such attachment to any earthly being as he had for Ann? He reflected bitterly also on his proud and ambitious nature, which had always been encouraged by his father. This pointed likewise to sinful self-centeredness. He forthwith launched an attack on what he considered the enemy of his soul, which encountered the threat of injury in the battle. He submerged himself in the writings that had long attracted him of the French mystic, Madam Guyon, along with those of Thomas à Kempis and Fenelon.

Judson broke all unnecessary social contacts, especially those with foreigners in general. He built a bambo hut for himself on the edge of the jungle, and there he meditated. He sometimes went to the Wades' house for meals; other times they sent meals to him. He reduced his own salary by one-fourth. In addition to giving to the mission the $2,000 or more he received for services to the commission negotiating a commercial treaty with Burma, he gave his life savings of $6,000 to the mission board.

Judson declined a doctor of divinity degree that was awarded him by Brown University. He destroyed correspondence files because some of the letters he had received expressed esteem and appreciation. He wished to make it as nearly impossible as he could for anyone later to say or write anything in his praise. He required of his sister in America that she destroy letters he had written home, refusing to sign a quit claim on inherited property until she did so.

For a period of six weeks Judson spent his days in prayer and moderate fasting by the ruins of an old pagoda in the tiger-invested jungle. At another period, in the effort to free himself from fleshly attachments, he sat for long hours beside an open grave reflecting on various stages of the body's decay and decomposition. Fortunately, this melancholia did not last very long.

One must not dwell too long on this unhappy period. It was not typical of the Adoniram Judson we know before and afterward. In 1629, during the period of disturbance, one of the resolutions he recorded was: "Believe in the doctrine of perfect sanctification attainable in this life." In later resolutions we do not find such statements. Rather, they emphasized a wholesome prayer life, maintaining a sweet spirit and doing good to others at every opportunity. The concluding point in one listing was: "Resolved, to make the desire to please Christ the grand motive of all my actions."

Even during the ascetic period—except for the six weeks in the jungle—Judson remained active in the mission. His regular reports to the board reveal continuous preaching, personal witnessing, and translation work—but no intimation of the struggles within. During the critical period—roughly two years from the time of the move to Moulmein in August 1827—Judson and Wade built up a church of fifty baptized Burmese members. Judson completed his revision of the New Testament and made progress on translation of the Old. He distributed thousands of tracts from his *zayat* and on the streets, and he prepared two new tracts. Not satisfied with these labors, he set out in 1830 on an evangelistic mission to the heart of Burma. This pioneer work may have marked the end to the period of unhealthy introspection.

Judson the Evangelist

Eager to undertake some pioneer missionary work, Judson went to Prome in Burma proper, about halfway up the Irrawaddy between Rangoon and Ava. The printer, Cephas Bennett, and his wife had come as new missionaries to Moulmein, and the Wades made an effort to revive the work in Rangoon. Judson consistently held to the conviction that missionaries should settle in as many strategic stations as possible rather than concentrate in one or two places.

Prome was a strategically located old town, dating from before the Christain era. Judson felt that a mission there might serve as a stepping stone to another effort in Ava. He had brought five Burmese Christians from Moulmein to work with him as evangelists in and around Prome.

At the beginning, authorities in Prome did not seem unfriendly. The people went in droves to request tracts from the missionary and hear what he had to say. Finding a place to live proved difficult, but the local authorities finally agreed for Judson to take over an old *zayat* and repair it to house his group. The mission team divided forces and went in different directions throughout town and into nearby villages, spreading the gospel by word of mouth and printed page. Within a few days most of the tracts that had been brought from Moulmein had been distributed, and Judson wrote to Bennett for more. Many people in the Prome area seemed to be considering Christianity as a way of life.

This encouraging period lasted only three weeks. The acting governor became cool, called Judson in for investigation, and reported to Ava. Judson wrote to fellow missionaries:

> Satan has industriously circulated a report that I am a spy in pay of the British. . . . All smiles and looks of welcome are passed away; people view me with an evil eye, and suffer their dogs to bark at me unchecked. . . . At Ava I have been regarded as a suspicious character ever since I deserted them at the close of the war and went over to the British.

Judson and his helpers labored three-and-a-half months in Prome, and there was only one surely-known convert, though the missionary felt there might be others. He wrote:

> There are some whose faces I expect to see at the right hand of the great Judge. There is no period of my missionary life that I review with more satisfaction, or rather with less dissatisfaction, than my sojourn in Prome.

Yet, at the time, there seemed to be no possibility of effective work. Judson left for Rangoon. (Actually, the king had already issued an order for his expulsion from Prome, but it had not reached local authorities.)

He spent the next ten months in Rangoon, where he majored on his first love—direct evangelistic work—although he labored too on the Old Testament translation. He rose at daybreak; took his morning walk and bath; then strolled along the streets, distributing tracts and speaking of the gospel to anyone who would listen. Every day there were conferences with those who came to his lodgings. "People find their way to me," he wrote, "from all parts of the country." He also directed the work of his several Burmese evangelists, as he had done in Prome.

As much as Judson enjoyed this work, it became necessary for him to return to Moulmein. He was the only available missionary who knew the language and the people well enough to direct the growing evangelistic and literary work there. Except for a few months, Moulmein was his home for the remainder of his life.

During the early years of the mission in Rangoon, Adoniram and Ann had seen from time to time small groups of wild-looking tribesmen pass along the road into the city. Inquiring about them, the missionaries learned they were Karens, regarded as much inferior by the Burmese. Judson discussed with Burmese converts the necessity of evangelizing these primitive people, who were numerous in the interior. The Karens seemed exceedlngly shy, however, and avoided contacts even with Burmese as far as possible.

Maung Shay Bay, a loyal believer and father of the two little girls the Judsons nurtured for several years, had encountered a Karen man after the war. His name was Ko (title for a mature or middle-aged man) Tha Byu, and he had led a life of crime—having been involved by his own count in thirty murders. Maung Shay Bay discovered that Tha Byu was for sale as a slave because of debt; Shay Bay paid the price for the release of the man. Remembering Judson's interest in the Karens, Shay Bay turned Tha Byu over to the missionary. Under Judson's instruction the man's irascible personality changed completely, and he became an earnest Christian.

Ko Tha Byu, despite his unpromising background, became an apostle to the Karens. Missionary Wade reduced their language to writing, and the Boardmans evangelized tirelessly among them.

The uncultured Karens were animists, without any well-established religion such as Buddhism was for the Burmese, yet proved to be much more open to the Christian gospel.

Within a month after his return to Moulmein in the summer of 1831, Judson entered the jungles on his first evangelistic tour among Karen villages. Although he had to work through an interpreter, he enjoyed much success. Forced back after a few weeks by attacks of fever, he brought with him three converts whom he began to instruct in a sort of adult Bible school he started in Moulmein. At the end of the year he and nine national helpers conducted a tour of ten weeks among the Karens that resulted in the baptism of at least twenty-five converts. A third Karen tour was likewise successful. This work in the jungle—traveling on foot from village to willage, preaching and dealing with inquirers, examining and baptizing converts—delighted Judson. Always a pioneer at heart, he regretted the necessity of literary and administrative responsibilities.

Adoniram and Sarah

George Boardman, beloved and successful missionary among the Karens, was worn with exhausting labors and died of tuberculosis early in 1831 while Judson was in Rangoon. Sarah Boardman refused to forsake the mission when her husband died. Although her own health was far from good, she never spared herself and traveled—often on foot and in all kinds of weather—among the Karen villages. This was in addition to her main work of conducting schools for girls in Tavoy.

Judson had been greatly admired by both of the Boardmans, and they named their second son after him and Wade. When Judson heard of Boardman's death he wrote a tender letter of condolence to Sarah. Among other considerate suggestions, he offered to make arrangements for the education of her small son George in America if she desired to send him there. Judson promised, in case anything happened to her, "to receive and treat him as my own son" if desired—little thinking at the time, apparently, that the boy would later be just about that.

Judson finished his translation of the Old Testament at the end of January 1834, having given himself almost exclusively to the task for the past two years. This was a great relief to him, a milestone in his missionary career. About this time, he allowed his thoughts to turn to more personal matters for a while.

He discovered that his affection for Sarah Boardman was not limited to his high regard for her as a loyal and dedicated missionary. The occasion for this train of thought may have been a letter that he received toward the end of Feburary, expressing appreciation for his excellent translation of the entire Bible into Burmese. For impulsive Adoniram, the proposal did not wait long after the discovery. As Sarah replied with a hearty yes, they married on 10 April. Adoniram was forty-five years-old, and his bride was fifteen years younger. Their union was a happy one for eleven years.

Sarah was an attractive and intelligent woman. Adoniram later regretted that there was no portrait of his second wife. He described her "soft blue eyes, her mild aspect, her lovely face and elegant form." As evidence of her intelligence, she learned the Karen (there were several), Talaing, and Burmese languages; translated several evangelistic materials into Talaing; and composed some original writing.

Soon after their marriage it became necessary to send George, Sarah's only surviving child, to America. He was only six years of age, but the Judsons regarded it as too risky to keep him any longer. Children of Western parents in that part of the world suffered from tropical diseases. Even those who lived were sometimes debilitated in mind or body. Adoniram loved George as his own son, and some of Judson's most appealing letters were written to him during the boy's schooldays in America.

Adoniram and Sarah's first child was born in October 1835. This only daughter was named Abigail (Abby Ann) after his mother, sister, and first wife. Seven sons were born to them within the next ten years; one was still-born, and two others died under the age of two. Every bereavement was a tragic loss for the Judsons.

Adoniram and Sarah experienced much joy with their children. It was the first chance for fairly normal family life that Adoniram had known, with children growing up around him. He was always an affectionate and considerate father as well as a loving husband. While absent from home, he wrote letters to Sarah and the children. He sometimes composed verses for the children and enclosed them with the letters. Two prayer quatrains exemplify these:

> Dear Jesus, hear me when I pray,
> And take this naughty heart away;
> Teach me to love Thee, gracious Lord,
> And learn to read Thy holy word.
>
> Come, dearest Saviour, take my heart,
> And let me ne'er from Thee depart;
> From every evil set me free,
> And all the glory be to Thee.

With his passion for thoroughness and completeness, Judson felt dissatisfied with his Bible translation. Almost immediately upon finishing it he set out on a complete revision, He labored more on this during the following six years than he had on the original. On 14 October 1840, he finished this work and submitted the last sheet to the printer. Thus he gave to Burma one of the finest Bible translations anywhere. It is still regarded as the basic Burmese Bible, having gone through revised editions.

In a letter to Adoniram's mother, Sarah described her husband's work during this period:

> Mr. Judson preaches *every* Lord's day to a crowded assembly and every evening to a congregation averaging thirty. We find our old chapel too small and are about having a new one erected. The native assistants go about the town every day preaching the Gospel, and Mr. Judson holds a meeting every morning before breakfast, when he listens to their reports, prays with them, gives them instruction, etc. Besides this, the care of the Burman church, nine in number, devolves upon him, as does all the revision, superintendence of the press, etc., etc., etc.

Judson wrote in 1837:

> My days are commonly spent in the following manner: the morning in reading Burman; the forenoon in a public *zayat*, with some assistant preaching to those who call; the afternoon in preparing or revising something for the press, correcting proof-sheets, etc.; the evening in

conducting worship in the native chapel and conversing with the assistants and other native Christians or inquirers.

Illnesses and Bereavement

Judson considered his health remarkably good compared with that of other Westerners living in the East. He attributed this largely to his lifelong habit, from Andover days, of taking a long and rigorous walk at about sunrise each morning—preferably to some hilltop—followed by a cold bath. If the weather prevented, he found some suitable exercise at home such as chopping wood. He took pride in the fact that with one or two exceptions he had already survived longer on the field than any other missionary in the East.

Beginning in 1829, however, he had suffered with low fever intermittently from November to March each year. By 1838 the attacks had become lighter, but in that year he contracted a painful and persistent cough, with inflammation of the throat and lungs, that made it impossible during long periods for him to speak above a whisper.

Since he could not preach during the bad periods, he worked fulltime on the Bible revision. He had long looked forward to the completion of this task that would free him for pioneer work. The throat disease seemed to preclude travel and preaching, and he felt obliged to undertake another literary effort for which he had no liking. For years his colleagues and the board had prevailed on him to prepare a dictionary of the Burmese and English languages that could facilitate the training of new missionaries. He delayed as long as he conscientiously could, feeling that this work was "unmissionary," but now at last with almost an "order" from the board to do so, he undertook it.

In an effort to overcome his ailment and at the insistence of the other missionaries, Judson took a trip to Calcutta in the early spring of 1839. Homesick for his family and somewhat recovered in health, he returned to Moulmein within a few weeks.

With the return of the rainy season, his physical trouble also returned in full force. Judson's colleagues urged him to spend a year or two in American to regain his health. The board sent him an official invitation to do so and to take his wife and children with him if desired. He declined because his health seemed slightly better at the time and without normal use of his voice, he felt he could be worth little to the mission cause in U.S. churches.

To a friend he wrote,

> My present expectation is to use medicinal palliatives, and endeavour to keep along for a few months until I see the present edition of the Bible completed. . . . But I shrink back again when I think of my dear wife and darling children, who have wound round my once widowed, bereaved heart, and would fain draw me down from heaven and glory. And then I think, also, of the world of work before me. But the sufficient answer to all is: "The Lord will provide."

He assumed he had tuberculosis, from which manissionaries in the East had died.

Judson's health improved enough for him to do some preaching from time to time, but he was never entirely free from the throat disease. Sarah's health seriously declined early in 1845. Her husband wrote to the Board:

> It is the unanimous opinion of all the medical men, and indeed of all our friends, that nothing but a voyage beyond the tropics can possibly protract her life beyond the period of a few weeks, but that such a voyage will, in all probabllity, insure her recovery.

Judson made the difficult decision to send her to America. He had hoped that she could travel alone, but she became so weak before passage could be arranged that he had to accompany her. The three youngest children—Henry, Charles, and Edward—were left with friends in Moulmein. The other three children—Abby Ann, young Adoniram, and Elnathan—were taken on the trip. Two Burmese assistants went also. Judson had been working hard on the dictionary for several years, and he desired to continue this work during the voyage and in the United States.

Sarah improved so much during the first stage of the voyage that Adoniram felt it his duty to return from the Isle of France. He sent his two literary assistants home on the first ship available from that place and intended himself to take the next one back to Burma. At this juncture his wife's health took a turn for the worse, and he left with her on another ship for the United States. She rallied several times but suffered a final relapse as they neared St. Helena and died while the ship was in harbor there on 1 September. She was buried on the island, and a grieving Adoniram reembarked with his three motherless children.

Sad of heart, he looked forward without enthusiasm to his first visit in America, which he had left thirty-three years before.

Visiting in the Old Homeland

Judson expected to remain only a short time in the United States. He wanted to get the three children suitably settled with relatives and friends and desired to confer with members of the mission board about the work in Burma. He looked forward to seeing his dear sister Abigail, comrade of his youth and faithful correspondent through the years. Others of the immediate family—father, mother, and brother Elnathan—were all deceased.

Most of the time while he was in America he expected to spend on the dictionary, and he bitterly regretted sending his assistants back. In a letter written shortly before leaving Moulmein he had explained to the secretary of the board why—in addition to his throat trouble—he would not be able to make speeches:

> In order to become an acceptable . . . preacher in a foreign language, I deliberately abjured my own. . . . For thirty-two years I have scarcely entered an English pulpit or made a speech in that language. From long desuetude I can scarcely put three sentences together [for a speech] in the English language. I must therefore beg the board to allow me a quiet corner, where I can pursue my work with my assistants undisturbed and unknown.

As soon as passage could be arranged, he desired to return to Burma.

The self-effacing missionary had no idea that he was a hero to Christians in America and could not possibly remain among them "undisturbed and unknown." As his ship arrived in Boston harbor, his principal concern was that he had made no arrangements for lodgings that night. A hundred families would have thrown open their homes and considered it an honor to have him and the

children as guests, but Judson did not dream that he was so wide-
ly known and respected.

On 17 October, the second day after arrival, a meeting took
place at the Bowdoin Square Baptist Church of Boston to welcome
the missionary. Although there had not been time for wide pub-
licity, interested persons filled the building to overflowing. The
president of the Board of Baptist Missions presided. He spoke of
Judson's work in Burma and of the appreciation and affection that
the people at home felt for him. Then Judson stood to make a brief
statement of thanks. He wanted to ask the prayers of Christians in
America for the work in Burma. His voice was so weak that one
of the local pastors stood at his side and repeated each sentence
after him so that the people could hear what the missionary said.

After Judson had finished his statemdnt, his "translator" began
with some remarks of his own. As he spoke, there was a commo-
tion among the people. A middle-aged or elderly man was making
his way to the front. Judson glanced at the gentleman, then stared
hard. It was Samuel Nott!

Judson had assumed that all members of his original band
were dead except for himself. The two men shook hands and then
embraced. Samuel Nott had been the one of their little pioneer
group of missionaries with whom Adoniram felt most intimate.
Nott had stood with him in forcing the American Board to effective action by giving notice that they would otherwise go out
under the British society. Nott had defended him when he became
a Baptist, while others assailed his integrity for making the change.
Nott's missionary career had ended in 1816 when ill health forced
him home. He then began service as a Congregational pastor in
Wareham.

Nott was introduced to the congregation, and he began to
speak with deep emotion. More than thirty years ago, he said, he
gave this brother "the right hand of fellowship, and when he became a Baptist it was not withdrawn." He recalled that except for
Judson and himself, all members of that original band were dead.
Soon they would be gone too, along with missionaries of other
agencies, but the word of God that was behind all they tried to do
would "stand fast and prevail over all the earth."

A special meeting of the Baptist mission board was called to honor Judson. After that service he visited Salem, Bradford, Brown University, and Plymouth. He arranged to leave his two little boys with friends in Worcester and Abby Ann with others. Calls came insistently from churches in various parts of the country, and Judson felt obliged to visit some of them. He traveled as far south as Richmond and would have gone farther if his poor health had not prevented it. The throat condition worsened, and only in the smallest groups could he speak without an "interpreter" to repeat his words for the assembly.

From Richmond he wrote to the president of the new Southern Baptist Convention, "This city I determined at all risks to visit in the welfare and prosperity of which I feel deeply interested. But farther south I *cannot.*"

J. B. Jeter, director of the new Foreign Mission Board, said at a meeting in Richmond to honor Judson:

> We have marked your labors, have sympathized in your various sufferings, have shed many a tear at the foot of the hopia tree, . . . the rocky island of St. Helena, have rejoiced in your successes . . . and have long and fervently wished to see your face. . . . We love you for the truth's sake and for your labors in the cause of Christ. We honor you as the father of American missions.

Judson in his response said:

> I congratulate the Southern and Southwestern churches on the formation of the Southern Baptist Convention for Foreign Missions. . . . Such an organization should have been formed several years ago. Besides other circumstances, the extent of the country called for a separate organization. I have read with much pleasure the proceedings of the convention at Augusta, Georgia, and commend the dignified and courteous tone . . . of that body. . . . If hereafter the more violent spirits of the North should persist in the use of irritating language, I hope they will be met, on the part of the South, with dignified silence.

From Richmond, Judson returned to the Northern states, where he took part in services in numerous churches. Since he was seldom able to speak directly to an assembly, he sometimes felt that he was on public display, and this irritated him exceedingly. Sometimes he seemed unresponsive and cool toward those who sought to meet him, especially if he suspected that they thought of him as a celebrity.

Some people were disappointed in his addresses. They wanted to hear about his exciting experiences. He preferred to speak about the great truths of the Gospel. He did emphasize the need for this Gospel in Burma as well as everywhere else and the need for more missionaries. Judson remained in America almost nine months, but he could not find time to work on the dictionary. His heart remained in Burma, and he wanted to return there as soon as possible. He discovered, however, that his heart was in a sense in America too.

Another Whirlwind Romance

On a cold December day Judson traveled by train from Boston to Philadelphia, where some mission meetings were to be held. He was accompanied by A. D. Gilette of Philadelphia. Suddenly the train came to an unexpected stop; an accident had occurred that would cause a delay of two or three hours. Dr. Gilette, desirous of providing some entertainment for the missionary during this time, borrowed a book that he saw in the hand of a friend and gave it to Judson.

He took the volume hopefully in hand, but his face fell as he read the title: *Trippings in Author Land*, by Fanny Forrester. He thought, "What kind of a book was that for a missionary?"— especially a missionary who had disciplined himself in Burma not to read anything in English except devotional materials and a single religious periodical. But after all, he was not in Burma, and there seemed nothing else to do during the delay. He read a few words here and there, then a few more, and soon seemed engrossed in the book. It was a series of sketches written in a light but attractive style.

Judson asked Gilette about the author. The pastor informed the missionary that she was a young woman who taught in a girls' school in Utica, New York and had achieved some popularity as a writer. Judson wanted to know whether she was a Christian. His friend replied that not only was she a Christian but a Baptist.

"I should be glad to know her," Judson declared. "The lady who writes so well ought to write better. It's a pity that such fine talents should be employed on such subjects."

Gilette replied with a wry smile that Dr. Judson would soon have the opportunity of meeting her, for she was a guest in his own home at the time.

Judson was being entertained in another home, but promptly the next morning he presented himself at the Gilette place. Fanny Forester, whose real name he learned was Emily Chubbock, was there, receiving a smallpox vaccination. She was not beautiful; her nose was rather large, and her lips were quite thin—but she was vivacious and cheerful, definitely an attractive person. Judson felt her charm at once.

As soon as the vaccination ordeal concluded, he said he would like to speak with her. Emily answered in a half-playful manner that she would be delighted and honored to be talked to by the missionary. Judson conducted her to a sofa and began with characteristic forthrightness to inquire "how she could reconcile it with her conscience to employ talents so noble in a species of writing so little useful or spiritual" as the sketches he had read.

This was such a question as would ordinarily arouse the fire of her spirit. As she looked into the earnest face of this man, however, her heart melted and she replied with seriousness and candor. Her indigent parents were dependent upon her for support, she said. Her more serious writings would not sell, but the frothy Fanny Forester sketches and longer works did. Anyway, she was careful to write nothing immoral or harmful, and she felt justified in satisfying the public taste in order to support her parents.

At that point, the sternness of the missionary melted. He admitted that the demands of filial love might justify such a course. Then he changed the subject. He wanted someone to prepare a memoir of his recently deceased wife Sarah, and it was mainly with this in mind that he had desired to make the authoress' acquaintance.

Emily expressed interest in the project, as no one was more eager than she that her talents be employed on worthy subjects. Judson found it necessary to have several long conferences with Emily to discuss the matter of preparing the memoir. On 5

January, eleven days after meeting her, Adoniram "began an acquaintance" with Emily Chubbock—that is, he made his intentions clear as a suitor.

On the twentieth day of the same month he sent his proposal—mainly in the form of what he called a "charmed watch." In an accompanying letter he explained,

> It always comes back to me and brings its bearer with it. I gave it to Ann . . . and it brought her . . . to my arms. I gave it to Sarah during her husband's lifetime (not then aware of its secret) and the charm, though slow in its operation, was true at last. . . . . . Should you . . . toss back the article, saying "Your watch has lost Its charm; it comes back to you, but brings not its wearer with it"—O first dash it to pieces, that it may be an emblem of what will remain of the heart of your devoted.
>
> A. Judson

Although a fifty-seven-year-old widower and America's senior missionary to the East, Judson made an irresistible suitor. He really seemed younger. His step was sprightly, his face smooth and rather youthful in appearance, his full head of chestnut hair unlined with gray, and his health good except for the throat ailment. Emily, not quite twenty-nine years-old, felt a rapidly deepening affection for hlm. She realized that it would be regarded as an unusual union, but there seemed to be no valid reason for not following the leading of their hearts. She kept the watch.

Upon the announcement of their engagement, a storm of disapproval arose, both from the literary world where Fanny Forester ranked as a rising favorite and from the church world where Adoniram Judson was a mission hero with a halo about his venerable head. Literary people thought the poor girl had been momentarily bewitched by this old man from the East, who was committing a crime to take her away from her reading fans into the wilds of an uncultured land.

Such opinions did not bother them much, but the bitter criticism of some church people were a different matter. Many held it to be incredible that Judson would marry such a woman of the world, the frivolous literary world. Eventually, this criticism made Emily most miserable, but it left Adoniron unperturbed. He despised the idolizing spirit anyway.

In a letter from Plymouth, written in April while the criticism was at its peak, he sought to comfort her with the assurance that "it will soon pass away." He noted with amusement how his children reacted favorably when they knew that papa was marrying Emily. Abby Ann had heard from neighbors that Papa's wife-to-be was Fanny Forester and felt sure that she must be a very good lady because she had written *Effie Maurice*, one of her favorite books.

The excitement soon ended, as Adoniram had predicted. The church people became reconciled when they learned that Emily was a devoted Christian. Years before, she had seriously considered becoming a missionary. Adoniram and Emily were married on 2 June 1846 at her parents' home in Hamilton, New York.

Back in the Real Homeland

Although urged to remain longer in America for the sake of his health, Judson determined to take the first available ship for Burma. From experience he knew that America was no place for a missionary to be cured of a throat disease because of being called on so often to speak. Anyway, he felt homesick for Burma and anxious to resume his work there.

Adoniram told Emily that he did not want her to feel unduly cramped as a writer because of her marriage to a missionary and that she could certainly continue to write as she wished. He paid off the mortgage on the home she had bought for her parents, repayment to be made from her future royalties. He visited publishers while he was in New York just before the wedding and made arrangements about her books.

Farewells were difficult for both of them. They had a few days at Hamilton with Emily's parents then visited in Plymouth and Bradford. Adoniram's sister, Abigail, locked his room at the old family homestead in Plymouth; it remained undisturbed, just as he had left it, until her death nearly forty years later. Adoniram made a quick journey to Worcester, Massachusetts for a last tearful farewell with his sons, young Adoniram and Elnathan, then on to Bradford for the same with Abby Ann.

The *Faneuil Hall*, on which passage had been secured, sailed for Moulmein 11 July. As Adoniram stood on the deck with Emily, waving to the hundreds on shore who had come to see them off, he realized that this would almost certainly be the last view of his native land. Still the invererate pioneer, with Emily at his side, he looked to the future. There was work to do for God, which he could do, and he felt eager to be at it.

After an enjoyable voyage of twenty weeks the Judsons arrlved in Moulmein on the last day of November 1846. Adoniram delighted in reunion with his two young sons, Henry and Edward (Charlie had died before his mother did), and his missionary colleagues. He proudly introduced Emily to them.

As much as Judson enjoyed working closely with the other missionaries, he was troubled by the fact that of the twenty-nine appointees of the board in Burma, twenty-four resided in Moulmein. None were in Burma proper. Although all were usefully employed—in the printing office, the schools, evangelistic work, among various nationalities—Judson felt that such a concentration of forces could not be justified.

He determined that something should be done about the problem, at least so far as his own work was concerned. He resolved to make a new trial in Burma proper, probably Rangoon. This would be in keeping also with his constant desire to do what he considered to be *real* missionary work. Even the labor on the dictionary might be done better in Rangoon than in Moulmein where there were fewer Burmese scholars to help.

He made a preliminary trip to investigate, then in February 1847 moved with Emily and his two young sons into the second floor of an old brick house he had rented in Rangoon. It was a cavernous and drafty place of about eight huge rooms but no glass windows, "as gloomy as a prison." Roaches, lizzards, ants, rats, and bedbugs abounded; a thousand or more bats inhabited the attic. Judson disliked bringing his wife and children into such quarters, but the mission house had been destroyed during the war, and this was the best he could do. Campaigns were launched on the insects from time to time, and hundreds of bats were killed —but their places were taken by others.

The residence was finally made livable, and Judson began his work. The governor of Rangoon seemed friendly and gave permission for the missionary to conduct services in English for foreign residents and to work on his English-Burmese dictionary. He knew very well that Judson wished to evangelize the Burmese, but this topic they avoided. The king and his government in Ava were hostile to such work and this point of view was well represented in Rangoon by the assistant governor—"the most ferocious, bloodthirsty monster" Judson had ever known in Burma. The governor manifested weakness in his administration, and this assistant exercised authority.

Judson wrote:

> Any known attempt at proselyting would be instantly amenable at the criminal tribunal and would probably be punished by the imprisonment or death of the proselyte and the banishment of the missionary. . . . The prospects of a missionary were never darker.

As soon as they were settled, Adoniram set to work on the dictionary, while Emily composed the memoir of Sarah and cared for the family as best she could. He reorganized the Burmese church in Rangoon and found that of twenty nominal members, only about half were faithful and courageous enough to make a new beginning. For their meetings on Sunday these few would come, one at a time—often disguised as servants, delivery boys, or workmen—and leave in the same way over a period of several hours. The worship services were held behind locked doors in the missionary quarters.

For three months the work continued in this way. Attendance at Sunday services increased to twenty-five or thirty, and several baptisms were administered in secret. On Friday, 28 May, the Rangoon government issued a private order to have the Judson place watched by police in order to arrest anyone who might be liable to the charge of favoring "Jesus Christ's religion." Adoniram received word of this order privately on Saturday and sent messengers to the homes of believers and friends to advise them not to attend services until further notice. The government then began to badger the Christians with petty annoyances, suggesting worse to come. One convert was arrested, but the case came to the attention of the governor, who released him.

The king recalled the tolerant governor of Rangoon to Ava, and the future of the mission became more unpromising than ever.

Judson continued to do what he could in private, but inquirers ceased to come. He decided once again on an appeal to Ava for toleration. Humanly regarded, it still seemed to be the only hope for establishing the work on a solid basis. Judson secured a permit from the Rangoon government for going to the "Golden Feet" and made necessary preparations. The board in America had approved the plan but made no specific appropriation for the undertaking.

The Judsons never considered that money would be lacking for this strategic move. Then a letter came from the missionaries in Moulmein, stating that the budget for work in Burma had been greatly reduced by the board, and the local mission must decide where retrenchment should be made. The missionaries in Moulmein felt they could not approve the needed funds for the trip to Ava. They allowed only seventeen-and-a-half rupees a month for Judson's work in Rangoon, while he paid eighty-six rupees for house rent and assistants alone.

This decision was an awful shock. Judson felt abandoned. Gradually, however, he regained his usual serenity. Somehow, he reasoned, it must be God's will. Calmly he described the situation to the mission secretary in the U.S.:

> Instead, therefore, of entering on a new and expensive undertaking, I find myself unable to remain in Rangoon . . . in present circumstances, unable to remain to any advantage without making friends at Ava. . . . There remains nothing for me but to fall back upon Moulmein.

For the sake of the family, it was probably best that they were obliged to leave Rangoon. All had been seriously ill, and there was no doctor in the town. Proper food could not be obtained. They had to live almost exclusively on boiled rice and fruits; these were often inedible. The only palatable meal they had for a long period of time consisted of rats, they afterward learned from the cook. One child had erysipelas and the other had a complication of diseases. Adoniram had violent attacks of dysentery that kept him from his study table for six weeks.

Emily wrote to a friend:

> For myself, I am utterly prostrated, and, although I have taken care of everything and written a little, I have not sat up an hour at a time for six

weeks. . . . Now, do you think I am in any way discontented or would go back to America to live in a palace? Not I. I am ten times happier than I could be there. . . . And then we are so, so happy in each other. . . . We are frequently startled by echoing each other's unspoken thought, and we believe alike in everything.

With insufficient funds for the work, the threat of serious persecution for converts, and the entire family ill—there seemed nothing else to do but to return to Moulmein. In addition, Emily was expecting a baby.

True Holiness Achieved

The Judsons finally found a vessel that could take them to Moulmein, and they embarked on the last day of August. After arrival and settling in there, the health of the family members rapidly improved. The baby, Emily Frances, was born on Christmas Eve 1847.

The picture we have of the Judsons during the ensuing period is one of quiet and contentment. Adoniram had general oversight of the mission, continued his labors on the dictionary, and was able to preach at least once a week in the Moulmein chapel. He continued as a sympathetic counselor for the younger missionaries and never lorded it over them.

Emily wrote in a letter home:

He "works like a galley slave," and really it quite distresses me sometimes, but he seems to get fat on it, so I try not to worry. He walks—or rather *runs*—like a boy over the hills, a mile or two every morning; then down to his books . . . so on till ten o'clock in the evening.

Home life was a joy to Adoniram, and he delighted to romp with the children. "We are a very happy family," he wrote to friends, "not a happier, I am sure on the broad earth." Nor did he forget the older children in America, to whom he wrote warm, fatherly letters. There were frequent references in conversation and correspondence to those who had died. Ann and Sarah were remembered, as Ann had been during his second marriage, in a warm and wholesome way that was fully shared by Emily.

Early in 1849 Judson finished the English-Burmese dictionary, and it was published in a quarto edition of about 600 pages. He turned his attention forthwith to the Burmese-English part, which he was not able to complete.

His chief concern was for his wife. He wrote to pastor Gilette:

> Emily's health is very delicate, her hold on life very precarious. Yet she may live many, many years. . . . And while she does live, she will be a blessing to all, whether near or remote. I never cease to thank God that I found her, accidentally, as it were, under your roof.

It was Adoniram himself who neared the end. Several weeks before the above writing to Gilette, he had arisen one night to help Emily with one of the children who was not well. The weather was damp and windy and he began to be chilled. He had a cold the next day but thought nothing of it. His condition grew steadily worse, however, and in November he felt obliged to lay aside his work and never regained strength enough to take it up again. His work was done.

On the doctor's advice, Judson undertook brief sea voyages, but they failed to bring relief. At times he seemed to improve—but not for long. He continued to decline; he realized that his life was drawing to a close and felt at peace with the thought.

Then he seemed to develop a will to live. He told his wife:

> I do not believe I am going to die. I should like to complete the dictionary. . . . Then after that all the plans that we have formed. Oh, I feel as if I were only just beginning to be prepared for usefulness.
>
> It is not because I shrink from death that I wish to live. Neither is it because the ties that bind me here, though some of them are very sweet, bear any comparison with the drawings I at times feel towards heaven, but a few years would not be missed from my eternity of bliss, and I can well afford to spare them, both for your sake and for the sake of the poor Burmans. I am not tired of my work, neither am I tired of the world; yet when Christ calls me home, I shall go with the gladness of a boy bounding away from his school.

That call was coming. The doctor advised a long sea voyage, declaring that there was no hope at all for recovery otherwise. Emily had him put on the ship, being unable to go with him because of her own weakness and the expectation of another baby in a few days. Their parting was difficult, but both felt strong in the Lord.

A young missionary, Thomas Ranney, and a servant accompanied him.

It was too late, however, even if the voyage might have been of some help earlier. Adoniram spoke to Ranny from time to time, but he often suffered great pain and grew steadily weaker. His last words, spoken to the Burmese servant while Ranny was out, were: "Take care of poor mistress." The pains seemed gone, and he slipped quietly away.

He had always loved the sea, and during the last illness he had more than once expressed to Emily a preference for burial at sea. The desire was fulfilled, soon after he breathed his last breath on the afternoon of 12 April 1850.

Personally and as a missionary, the basic element in the life of Adoniram Judson surely was his devotion to Jesus Christ and the interests of the kingdom of God.

He said to a student missionary group during the visit in the United States,

> Let not your object be so much to "do your duty" or even to "save souls," though these should have a place in your motives, as to please the Lord Jesus. Let this be your ruling motive.

As to how one is to please Him, he went on,

> How, indeed, shall we know what will please him, but by *his commands*? Obey these commands and you will not fail to please him. And there is that "last command," given just before he ascended to the Father, "Go ye into all the world, and preach the gospel to every creature." It is not *yet* obeyed as it should be. Fulfill that, and you will please the Saviour.

Judson felt strongly that the decision to become a missionary was a lifelong commitment. He wrote to the mission board secretary:

> If the limited-term system, which begins to be fashionable in some quarters, gain the ascendancy, it will be the death blow of missions and retard the conversion of the world a hundred years. . . . The motto of every missionary—whether preacher, printer, or schoolmaster—ought to be: "Devoted for life."

Certainly this was the motto for the missionary, Adoniram Judson.

Note on Sources

Anderson's biography of Judson is the best in its class—quite complete, readable, and useful. Quotations come mostly from the works by Wayland and Edward Judson. The other quotations are taken from Knowles and the writings of Ann and Emily Judson.

Selected Bibliography

Anderson, Courtney. *To the Golden Shore: The Life of Adoniram Judson*. Boston: Wittle, Brown, and Company, 1956.

Hall, Gordon Langley. *Golden Boats from Burma*. Philadelphia: Macrae Smith, 1961.

Hubbard, Ethel Daniels. *Ann of Ava*. New York: Friendship Press, 1941.

Judson, Ann H. *An Account of the American Baptist Mission to the Burman Empire in a Series of Letters Addressed to a Gentleman in London*, 1827.

Judson, Edward. *The Life of Adoniram Judson*. Philadelphia, 1883.

Knowles, James D. *Memoir of Mrs. Ann H. Judson, Wife of the Rev. Adoniram Judson, Missionary to Burma*. London, 1829.

McElrath, William N. *To Be the First: Adventures of Adoniram Judson, America's First Foreign Missionary*. Nashville: Broadman Press, 1976.

Pearn, B. R. *Judson of Burma*. London: Edinburgh House Press, 1955.

Warburton, Stacy R. *Eastward, the Story of Adoniram Judson*. New York: Round Table Press, 1937.

Wayland, Francis. *A Memoir of the Life and Labours of the Rev. Adoniram Judson, D.D.*, 2 volumes. London, 1853.

Luther Rice—
Man Of Vision and Toil

Luther Rice pioneered in religious journalism and higher education and brought Baptists of the United States together as a mission agency and denomination. Many of his contemporaries, even Baptist leaders, failed to comprehend his vision or give him the credit he deserved. Some of them could see only his weaknesses and failures. He traveled incessantly, drove himself mercilessly, worked for years without salary, took blame that should have been shared by others, and died at the age of fifty-three while on a fundraising tour in southern states.

A Purposeful Youth

The youngest son of a former captain in the Revolutionary army, Luther was born in the Massachusetts village of Northborough on 25 March 1783. He had six older siblings and a younger sister, and three others died early in life. When he was age six, President George Washington visited Northborough. The boy's father rode at the head of the presidential parade through the village.

Typical of the many Rices in the area, Luther grew to be a tall and stalwart youth, musical and fun-loving. He attended the one-teacher village school and became a voracious reader. At the age of sixteen, without consulting his parents, he signed on for a lumbering expedition to Georgia to secure timber for shipbuilding. This work lasted about six months.

The elder Rices held membership in the local Congregational church, at that time the established state church in Massachusetts. Luther's father, Amos, evidently made no profession of personal religious experience and had the reputation of a rather heavy drinker. Luther was christened as an infant and through the years attended church with the other family members. When he was eighteen he came under conviction for his sins and, at Peter Whitney's suggestion, attempted to deal with the problem by becoming —somewhat earlier than usual—a full member of the church.

Luther still did not experience peace to his spirit. For over three years, a considerable part of his time and energies were seemingly spent in soul-searching and self-reproach as he implored God for salvation. He listened to the sermons of ministers in towns nearby, read several books of devotion, and agonized in pleading prayer. Luther's father ridiculed him for the seriousness with which he sought God. John Robinson, minister in Westborough, advised him to disregard his own feelings, act on the teachings of scripture, and leave the rest to the Lord.

Eventually, on a Saturday in September 1805, peace finally came. In his personal journal that day Luther wrote that the thought had come to him, "whether I would be willing to give Deity a blank and let Him fill up my future destiny as He should please!" He felt able to respond positively and wrote, "I would give God a blank to fill for me." That evening he went to his room and made the full commitment. "I did then on my bended knee give of myself to the eternal Jehovah, soul and body, for time and eternity to be dealt with as He should see fit." Doubtings as to his salvation seemed never to assail him after that.

Meanwhile, he worked on his father's farm and helped out from time to time on his brother's farm nearby. Luther's parents evidently expected that he as the youngest son would manage the home place when they were no longer able to do so. Perhaps to encourage this, Amos Rice gave Luther a horse and the deed to forty acres of his land.

Even before he found spiritual peace, Luther had been thinking that if God ever did save him, he would like to become a minister. This meant more education. His father gave permission for him to attend a small local academy, where he studied for the last two years of the existence of the institution—that is, when he was not too busy on one of the farms. Luther also attended singing schools, exercising and training his fine voice, and continued extensive reading.

Next he attended an academy in the village of Leicester, just over twenty-five miles from Northborth borough, for most of two years. School terms were short, and to pay expenses Luther taught school in the village of Paxton, just north of Northborough. His duties as a teacher included conducting singing schools and the village choir. In these he used to advantage his good voice, pitch pipe, and flute.

Still Luther worked much of the time on the farms. During periods in Northborough he began conducting prayer meetings in homes and schoolhouses. Pastor Peter Whitney objected, however, and homes that had been open to Luther and the little groups of people who attended were no longer available. One exception was that his brother, Asaph—although he did not participate—continued to allow the meetings in his home. He gave both moral and financial support in Luther's later undertakings as well.

Asaph bought the forty acres of land that had been given to his brother three years before, engaging to pay $900 for it in installments. Thus Luther was assured funds for completing a college education.

The Mission Volunteers

Luther was admitted as a sophomore in the fall of 1807 at Williams College in the Berkshire Mountains, just inside Massachusetts on the northwest corner. Living conditions at the college were Spartan. Students brought their water from a spring, cut wood, and built their own fires. Boardinghouses in town furnished meals at nine or ten shillings (then just over two dollars) a week. In the first year students studied mainly English, Latin, and Greek—with logic, rhetoric, and mathematics added the next year. Luther was a good student.

Although outstanding in music and public speaking, his main extracurricular activity during college and seminary years was with a group of serious-minded mission volunteers in a secret society named "the Brethren." The society's prime mover was Samuel Mills, whose appearance and personality contrasted sharply with Luther's. Mills was described by some of his contemporaries as small in stature and awkward in movement, with a hoarse and discordant manner of speaking. He fell far short in academic achievement.

Actually Samuel Mills started with a dream and attracted superior men to it. At Williams College, a year before Luther entered, Mills had led a small group of fellow students in the "haystack prayer meeting" for foreign missions. Later he organized the Brethren society, which had only four other members when Luther joined.

The society was kept secret to avoid too much criticism, especially from extreme Calvinists who objected to the rashness of young enthusiasts presuming to interfere with the elections of Providence by endeavoring to convert people in unevangelized areas. The students were concerned also, in case their project should fail, that this might bring reproach on the great cause of missions.

The constitution of the society was written in cipher for reasons of secrecy. All members were committed to go out as missionaries unless providentially prevented. They obligated themselves to remain always ready to embark on mission anywhere, at the discretion of the Brethren society, not taking on responsibilities that could prevent this. Marriage was excluded at first, but this rule changed.

Mills gave so much time to conversations about missions and the seeking of volunteers that he neglected college studies. He barely managed to finish the courses, and grades were so low that the faculty did not permit him to take part in graduation exercises. When he left Williams in 1809, leadership of the Brethren fell to Luther Rice. Luther wrote to his brother Asaph, "I have deliberately made up my mind to preach the gospel to the heathen, and I do not know but it may be Asia."

By the time Rice enrolled at Andover Theological Seminary in 1810, Mills was there and had established the Brethren society. Adoniram Judson had graduated but remained in the area and was working with the Brethren. Andover was a new institution, having completed only two sessions. Conservative Congregationalists, troubled about liberalism at Harvard, had established it.

Student life at Andover, as at Williams, was austere. The students chopped their wood and drew their water. The dining room was unheated. The Paul Revere bell called everyone to chapel at seven in the morning and at six o'clock in the summer.

Luther joined the seminary choir and plunged with zeal into biblical studies. Because he had been licensed to preach, he frequently traveled by his horse and chaise to supply in pulpits nearby.

In their planning for foreign missions, the little group of volunteers approached influential pastors and seminary professors for advice. One of the professors, Moses Stuart, invited five ministers of the area to meet with the volunteers in his home on Monday, 27 June 1810. The Brethren chose Samuel Newell, a self-effacing member of their group, to present the case of those offering themselves as missionary candidates. They considered Mills and Rice too aggressive for this delicate task.

After the presentation and discussion it was suggested that the young men prepare a "memorial" for the annual meeting of the association of the churches meeting in Bradford two days hence. Six men desired appointment, but Professor Stuart considered this too large of a number to make the original petition. He believed the delegates might be frightened from taking any positive action if so many seemed to be seeking support. The names of Luther Rice and one other person, both undergraduates, were dropped.

Adoniram Judson and three Samuels—Newell, Nott, and Mills —presented their appeal to the association. They were heard with great interest, and the decision was made to establish a "Board of Commissioners for Foreign Missions." The volunteers were told to continue preparing themselves and await developments.

Making It to India

While a student at Williams College, Luther had visited in the home of a fellow-student, William Eaton of Framingham. Luther felt attracted to Rebecca, the second daughter of four in that home. He continued seeing her at every opportunity. This was not difficult during Andover days, for Rebecca taught school just over twenty miles from the seminary. Late in 1810 they became engaged.

Surely Rebecca knew of Luther's burning passion for missions, but she evidently did not realize that it was a firm commitment. If she did, she must have regarded it as an enthusiasm that would pass. Luther had received a good education and shone among students as a rising pulpiteer. Rebecca probably surmised that he would settle as the pastor of some influential church. In any case, she evidently declined to go overseas as the wife of a missionary. This crushed Luther. He continued to see Rebecca, trying to get her to reconsider, but she stuck by her decision.

He completed his studies at the seminary in September 1811 but remained in the area preaching and teaching. He maintained contact with the Brethren.

Judson, and to some extent Nott also, threatened to accept appointment under the Congregationalist London Missionary Society unless the American board met their request. The board finally voted in September to appoint Judson, Nott, Newell, and Gordon Hall "as missionaries to work in Asia, either in Burma . . . or elsewhere, as . . . Providence might open the door." Mills wished to be appointed too, but the other brethren considered him less qualified than the scholarly Gordon Hall.

Board leaders, seminary students, and others busied themselves promoting the mission project and seeking funds. They raised enough money through gifts and borrowing to send the new missionaries to their destination. Plans were made for the ordination of the four candidates and their voyages overseas later.

Suddenly, Luther made up his mind to try to leave with the first group of missionaries, waiting no longer for Rebecca. The board's prudential committee would not take responsibility for appointing Rice on the same level as the others; he was required to raise money for his passage and living allowance until he could be appointed by the board in regular session. The committee's decision came only eleven days before the time set for the ordination and farewell service.

Rice wrote later: "I had to provide by begging funds for my outfit, passage etc." Negotiations with the committee and other business left "only six days to provide the necessary funds." He hit the road and worked day and night, soliciting support from individuals as well as churches and reached the needed amount barely in time. Luther's brother Asaph gave fifty-six dollars. Exhausted at the end of the money-raising ordeal, Rice wrote, "By the signal aid of providence, this was effected."

The ordination service took place on 6 February and lasted from 11 A.M. to 3 P.M. About 2,000 people packed the Tabernacle church in Salem. The wives of two of the candidates sat with them. Nott would be married two days later. Hall and Rice were single. Many addresses were delivered, and the five men received ordination. The society's corresponding secretary, Dr. Samuel Worchester, declared that this dedication of the new missionaries was "an act of our hearts."

The Judsons and Newells were scheduled to embark from Salem; the Notts, Hall, and Rice would sail on the *Harmony* from Philadelphia. After delays of many weeks, the *Harmony* finally set sail on 24 March 1812, five days after the *Caravan* had departed.

War clouds darkened between Britain and the U.S. Sea voyages were perilous, for "Britannia ruled the waves." Thirty-nine persons were aboard the *Harmony*, most of them crew and cargo-handlers, but passengers included two groups of British missionaries—a couple and a single woman of the London Missionary Society and two couples of the Baptist Missionary Society. The all-powerful East India Company forbade missionaries in its territories and usually succeeded in preventing British ships from transporting them, so some traveled by way of America.

One of the English Baptist missionaries was quite argumentative, particularly on the discussion of baptism between him and Rice. Rice, having grown up in New England Congregationalism, defended infant baptism as the equivalent of circumcision in the Old Testament. The Britisher emphasized the meaning of *baptizo* in the New Testament and even loaned Rice some books on baptism and the church.

Rice had known a few Baptists in his youth, although they had no church in his village. He regarded them as a spiritual people. In seminary he was distressed to be assigned the negative side in a debating exercise on infant baptism and was even more distressed to discover scripture based arguments against it. He intended to pursue the subject but never found the time until he was thrown together for months with the contentious English Baptist during the sea voyage.

Rice proved to be a poor sailor and was seasick much of the time. There was no heat in the cabins. Foul smells came from below-deck and food was uninviting. Despite all of this, he generally maintained his characteristic good humor. He played the flute, read, wrote in his personal journal, and talked with the Notts and Hall or other missionaries. On his twenty-ninth birthday he wrote in his journal,

> Various and singular vissitudes have I passed through the last year particularly in regard to a connection with _____ [Rebecca] and respecting missions.

He prayed, as recorded in his journal, "O Lord, pardon me and my problem heart."

The *Harmony* spent nearly a month in Port Louis, Isle of France (Mauritius). A company chaplain from India, on the Isle of France for his health, strongly advised against the missionaries' going to India or any territory under the East India Company. They continued on their voyage to India, however, and reached Calcutta on 10 August, four and one-half months after embarking from Philadelphia. The Judsons and Newells had landed about six weeks earlier. The authorities there told them they must leave. The Newells had already departed for the Isle of France. The captain of the *Harmony* was ordered to take Rice and the other missionaries back to Philadelphia. First, however, the captain needed to sell the cargo he had brought from America.

Change of Affiliation

Rice moved into the home of Mr. and Mrs. Rolt in Calcutta, where the Judsons already resided. Mrs. Rolt's deceased husband had been a British Baptist missionary and left many books on baptism and the church. Rice read extensively on these subjects while he was ill with hepatitis and had to stay indoors most of the time.

Rice attempted to draw Judson into a discussion of baptism, but Judson did not want to influence his friend unduly. He told him just to read the New Testament—and Judson's recently-printed sermon on the subject, if he desired. Rice, on his own request, received some help from the English Baptist missionary William Carey regarding the translation of New Testament passages relating to baptism. The seeking missionary wrote to his brother Asaph:

It is a principle with me that truth can be no loser by the most rigorous examination. May the Lord Himself lead me in the way in which He would have me to go.

Soon he felt he had that leading and wrote to the secretary of the American Board "informing him, and thereby the Board, of my late change of sentiment upon the subject of baptism." He explained his new conviction "that those persons only, who give credible evidence of piety are proper subjects and that immersion is the only proper mode of Christian baptism." Rice requested baptism and received it at the hands of English Baptist missionary William Ward at Lal Bazar Chapel in Calcutta on 1 November.

Several times the American missionaries thought they had passage to the Isle of France or some other place, but these hopes came to nothing. Police gave a new order that the Notts, Judsons, Hall, and Rice be shipped to England in a fleet that was prepared to leave. Reports had reached India of the outbreak of hostilities in the War of 1812 between Britain and the U.S. Local authorities were suspicious of all Americans. The Notts and Hall quickly secured passage to Bombay. They had heard that the governor there was tolerant of missionaries. They managed to elude police and hide on a vessel that took them there.

The Judsons and Rice evaded Calcutta police also, seeking passage on *La Belle Creole* for the Isle of France. A judge promised the necessary passes, then refused them, then promised and refused again. The three missionaries dared to place their baggage on board, still hoping for the passes. They embarked and the captain set sail downriver, only to be intercepted some hours later and ordered to shore for taking passengers who had been remanded to England.

The missionaries hid on shore while the vessel was searched. Rice, still quite ill, made a hurried trip to Calcutta to try again for the passes, which were again refused. He returned to the Judsons, then made another trip to Calcutta to seek the papers for passage —even if only to Ceylon (Sri Lanka)—but all was in vain. Reunited with the Judsons, Rice was having supper with them when someone handed him an envelope. It mysteriously contained the needed passes for the Isle of France.

Meanwhile, their baggage had been removed and the *Creole* sailed on down the coast. The missionaries made a dash for it and overtook the vessel before it headed into open sea. They boarded gratefully with their baggage. The ensuing seven-week voyage cemented the already cordial relationship between the Judsons and Rice. Adoniram was often despondent, but Luther maintained a cheerful and hopeful spirit, even when he was ill. He lightened some of the hours with singing or playing his flute.

When the ship docked at Port Louis, Samuel Newell went aboard and sobbed out a narrative of anguish: Enroute from India on a leaky vessel, Harriet—barely nineteen—had given birth prematurely to a baby girl on the floor of the cabin, attended only by her husband. The baby died and, soon after their arrival in Port Louis, Harriet died also. Samuel Newell, in deep sadness, departed for Bombay to join the missionaries.

The Judsons and Rice did not know whether Baptists in America would support them. Carey and Judson had written to Baptist ministers in the U.S., but had received no reply. The Serampore missionaries were providing funds to the three new Baptists for their travel and other expenses. As to their field for mission work, almost every door seemed closed, and even Carey feared that they would not be able to establish a mission in the East.

Rallying American Baptists

As the three discouraged missionaries discussed the problems, they decided that someone should return to America to make contacts with Baptists. This person should ascertain the feelings of fellow believers as to their support, help organize them for the purpose if this seemed avisable, then return to the mission station wherever it had been established. Because Rice was single, he was obviously the one for this service, plus in the U.S. he could receive better treatment for his liver complaint. Rice thought he might possibly persuade Rebecca to return to the field with him.

At the Isle of France he was already more than a fourth of the way to America from where the missionaries had been in India, and passage was available on the *Donna Maria*, via Brazil. Parting from the Judsons was difficult, for the three had become very close. Rice eagerly agreed to rejoin them in a few months, two years at the very most.

From St. Salvador, Brazil the *Donna Maria* was to proceed to Salem, Massachusetts, but its captain would not take Rice on this last part of the voyage. He had on board a quantity of saltpeter, which was contraband, and did not trust the minister missionary to lie in case of search to save the cargo. Finally, after two months in St. Salvador, Rice secured passage to New York, where he was warmly welcomed by Baptist churches.

Before attending to mission business with Baptists, however, he wanted to clear matters with the Congregationalists who had sent him to the mission field. Within a few days of arrival in the U.S. he appeared before the American Board of Commissioners for Foreign Missions, spoke for ninety minutes, and placed in secretary Worcester's hands a formal statement concerning his change to the Baptist position. He received no response from the board and was dismissed from the meeting.

Some members of the American Board deigned to converse with him privately a few days later. They told him the board had voted to consider the relation with Rice dissolved and desired that Rice refund the money expended for his outfit and passage to India. This seemed unreasonable to him since he had raised this money himself across denominational lines.

Rice began formal contacts about Baptist mission work with Thomas Baldwin, pastor of Boston's Second Baptist Church, and Lucius Bolles, a pastor in Salem. Bolles had attended the ordination service of the outgoing Congregationalist missionaries more than a year and a half before. There were local Baptist mission societies in Boston, Salem, and elsewhere. These included churches of the Philadelphia Baptist Association, America's oldest association, which commissioned Rice to visit churches and seek cooperation in the calling of a convention to set up a federation of mission societies. This assignment was the beginning of what proved to be his all-inclusive ministry among Baptists in the U.S. for the remainder of his life.

Rice planned travel also in the southern states, where more Baptists lived than in the North. He saw the importance of tapping this source and broadening the vision of the churches. Such an extensive operation had not been anticipated by mission-minded Baptists in Massachusetts and the Philadelphia association, though estimates of the number of Baptists in the entire nation at the time varied between 100,000 and 200,000.

This enthusiastic pioneer left Boston on 20 September, three weeks after his return from overseas. He visited briefly in his hometown then proceeded to New York City, Philadelphia, Washington, Richmond, Raleigh, Charleston, Augusta, and other points. In Washington City—as the capital was often called at the time—he addressed Congress, some members of which slipped a total of sixty-seven dollars into his pockets afterward.

Rice traveled in the beginning by public conveyance—stagecoach or boat—then turned almost exclusively to riding horseback or in a chaise he secured in Charleston, South Carolina. He often covered forty or fifty miles a day—and once ninety-three! Some of his annual reports indicate travel of 6,000 to over 9,000 miles a year. This travel was in addition to conferences with church leaders everywhere and interviews with well-to-do prospective donors for missions and constant preaching—in churches, outdoors, and in associational and other meetings.

The immediate task remained of enlisting support for a proposed convention in Philadelphia of delegates from mission societies. Rice organized many new local mission societies. Wherever he had a service—even in non-Baptist churches—he took an offering for missions.

He lived on the road, spending nights in homes of church members or inns. (He never had a home in the usual sense of the word.) He cemented lasting friendships, such as that with Dr. William Staughton, who as a student had taken part with William Carey and a few others in forming the original Baptist Missionary Society in Kettering, England in 1792. Other close associates included Obadiah Brown of Washington, Dr. Richard Furman of Charleston, and Jesse Mercer of Georgia.

Organizing for Missions

The Philadelphia convention began on Wednesday, 18 May 1814, and continued for more than a week. The first sessions were at

First Baptist Church, where physically-huge pastor Henry Holcombe welcomed delegates. They numbered thirty-three and represented missionary societies in various parts of the country. A third of the men were foreign-born or foreign-trained, indicating perhaps something of the need for strengthening indigenous organizations and institutions. Guests enlarged the assembly somewhat, but this gathering that started Baptist work on a national level was rather small.

Rice alone knew all the delegates and the societies they represented. He had led in the enlistment of the leaders and organization of the societies. During the convention he worked, mainly behind the scenes, to keep things moving. Richard Furman of Charleston was elected president. One important question to be decided was whether the general society or convention to be formed should devote itself to foreign missions exclusively or include home missions, ministerial education, and publications. Rice, supported by Furman and others from the South, preferred the more inclusive purpose and program. When the constitution was adopted, however, it provided only for foreign mission work.

The overall organization was named the General Missionary Convention of the Baptist Denomination in the United States of America for Foreign Missions. It was scheduled to meet every third year and thus became known as the Triennial Convention. It would be made up of individual mission societies and other Baptist organizations that contributed as much as $100 a year to the general mission fund. Twenty-one commissioners "who shall be members of paid societies, churches, or other religious bodies" would make up the executive body, which was named the Baptist Board of Foreign Missions for the United States.

The board elected Dr. Baldwin of Boston as its president and Dr. Staughton as corresponding secretary. It voted that

> Mr. Rice be appointed, under the patronage of this board, as their missionary to continue his itinerant services in these United States for a reasonable time, with a view to excite the public and more generally engage in missionary exertions and to assist in originating societies, or institutions, for carrying the missionary design into execution.

Rice's salary was set at eight dollars a week plus expenses. Another vote established that Judson "be considered as a missionary, under the care and direction of this Board" and that his support be assumed.

Staughton wrote soon afterward of Rice, while the latter was a guest in his home:

> He is a man of considerable talents—a good scholar, of an easy, popular pulpit address. His spirit is Catholic. but in relation to what he values truth or duty, he is firm. . . . He knows how to bear indignity without resentment, and fatigue without complaining.

Staughton thus gave a partial but rather good characterization of Rice, who would certainly have need of those qualities in the difficult tasks of organization and fund-raising he undertook.

As he traveled by chaise and on horseback, Rice distributed to key persons hundreds of copies of each annual report of the mission board, preached constantly, took mission collections, sought volunteers to work with the Judsons in Burma and enlisted home missionaries—especially for the central and western areas of the United States.

The best known home missionaries were John Mason Peck in St. Louis and Isaac McCoy, noted for his work among American Indians. In 1817 the second Triennial Convention amended its constitution to give the board "full power at their discretion to appropriate a portion of the funds to domestic missionary purposes." The home mission workers then received formal appointment under the board for their activities.

In the early years of his itinerating Rice spoke and wrote frequently about his return to the foreign mission field. The matter was discussed regularly at meetings of the board, which always asked him—although not unanimously—to remain in the U.S. a while longer. He became more and more involved in "holding the ropes" in the homeland, helping Baptists organize for maximum use of their resources and personally raising funds for the work at home and abroad.

For a time the principal reason Rice gave for not departing immediately for Burma—one for which he was ridiculed by critics —was that he needed to find a suitable wife to accompany him.

(Rebecca had refused to reconsider her decision and pursued a useful career in teaching and editorial work.) Later on, Rice's main reason for remaining in the U.S. was surely the manifold tasks he had taken in national Baptist development. He must have felt that these programs would fail if he abandoned them, which—in regard to the funding of some of them—was probably true.

Urgent appeals came regularly from Adoniram and Ann Judson for Luther to join them. They saw in him the best possible co-worker for the field in Burma; he was intellectual, lively, optimistic, musical, patient, and strong. The Judsons used every argument they could muster: the commitment made at their parting at the Isle of France, his suitability for foreign work, and the certainty they felt that there would be others to take his place for tasks in the homeland.

Manifold Undertakings

By 1817 Rice was enveloped in programs of support for foreign and home missions, a denominational paper, and then educational work. He wrote to Judson that he would need a decade to complete his task in the U.S. As Staughton strongly emphasized the need for Rice in America, Judson finally acquiesced, but appeals still came periodically from him and Ann to join them. Rice and Judson continued correspondence as long as Rice lived. The friend in the U.S. sent books and periodicals to the one in a faraway land. After hearing of Rice's death, Judson named his next son Luther, but the child was stillborn.

To give information about the various mission projects, Rice prevailed on the mission board to back the publication of a monthly periodical, *Latter Day Luminary*, which began in 1818 and soon had a circulation of eight thousand. It incorporated the board's *Annual Report*. Four years later Rice started a weekly paper, the *Columbian Star*, which was devoted primarily to foreign missions and educational ventures that were advocated by Rice.

He developed a deep conviction, even in early years of travel among the churches, that the greatest need of Baptists was dedicated and trained leadership. This spawned the dream for a great national Baptist university in Washington. Most of the churches, especially in the South and West, had ministers with little formal education. Many Baptists, notably in Kentucky and farther west, opposed the very idea of an educated and paid ministry. Even before 1820 Rice had begun speaking on education as he visited churches and associations, and he took collections for that purpose as well as for missions.

The Triennial Convention of 1817 voted, along with the admission of domestic missions as a valid concern of the body, a second amendment to its constitution stating that

> when competent and distinct funds shall have been received for the purpose, the board from these, without resorting at all to mission funds, shall proceed to institute a classical seminary.

Dr. Staughton in each of his pastorates had conducted in his home a seminary class for aspiring young ministers. The Board of Missions assumed the support of this work, naming Staughton as seminary principal and Irah Chase as instructor to assist him. Soon the number of students increased to twenty. Rice, acting for the school's board of trustees of which he was a member, purchased a forty-six-acre lot in Washington in 1820 and erected on it a five-story brick building and houses for the president and college steward.

Practically all funds for Columbian College, as it was named, were raised by Rice. Unfortunately, in the process, huge debts were incurred. The Triennial Convention, in approving the project in the spring of 1820, specifically directed those persons responsible "not to incur expenses beyond the amount of funds that may be obtained for the establishment."

The theological school of the institution opened in Washington in the fall of 1821. A medical department was added in 1825 and one for law in the following year. By 1824 there were ninety-three students representing twenty-one of the twenty-four states in the union at that time. Presidents, cabinet members, and other national government personalities supported the college and attended graduation exercises and ceremonial events. John Quincy Adams made a loan of $20,000, for which he eventually accepted $13,000 as repayment in consideration of the extreme financial distress of the institution.

In 1823 the Triennial Convention named a committee to investigate the indebtedness of Columbian College. The committee gave warnings but found no solution. Despite the warnings no retrenchment became evident. The college's trustees appealed to Congress for aid. A bill was introduced to that end, but Congress adjourned before it could be acted on—to the relief of Baptists who valued traditional principles of separation of church and state.

Unbelievable as it seems, announcement was made in 1824 that construction had begun on another college building as large as the existing one. It is not known who was chiefly responsible for this folly in the midst of the institution's disastrous financial condition. As usual, Rice alone received the blame. He did not protest this, although he could have justifiably done so. The building plans had to be cancelled, the unfinished structure remaining as a monument of frustration.

Buffeted by Brethren

Luther Rice believed that strong Baptist work at home and abroad required a great center for all programs. The logical place seemed to be the nation's capital. The establishment of Columbian College and the two periodicals in Washington were parts of this plan. Rice regretted that a new Baptist Tract Society, predecessor of American Baptists' Publication Society and Judson Press, was moved from Washington to Philadelphia.

The 1826 Triennial Convention, meeting in New York City, moved the mission board to Boston and again restricted itself to foreign missions as at the beginning. Sad as these developments were for Rice, sadder ones followed. A committee investigated the finances of the college and charged Rice with full responsibility for overspending, ignoring the part other college trustees had taken in all major decisions.

The committee searched but could find "nothing affecting the moral character of Mr. Rice . . . unless a want of punctuality in complying with his contracts be considered of that nature; and to that he pleads inability." It was charged that

the injunction of the Convention not to increase the debt was so far dis-
regarded as to go on with the business upon subscription instead of
money in hand. As the subscriptions were not collected as fast as the
money was wanted, a debt of fearful amount was contracted that has
since accumulated.

The report of the committee concluded:

In all these transactions, however, your committee can take pleasure in
stating that they see nothing like corruption, or selfish designs; although
he had fallen; into imprudences of very distressing tendency, he does not
seem to have any other object in view than the prosperity of the college.

Luther Rice was censured, stripped of his offices as agent of
the board and treasurer for the college. The convention then re-
nounced any connection with Columbian College and gave its full
attention to foreign missions.

Some persons who attacked Rice evidently hoped and expected
that this would strike the death knell of Columbian College, but it
did not—at least for the immediate future. Rice was bitterly attacked during this period in the *Columbian Star*, which he had
established and funded. He protested this indignity to Obadiah
Brown, who served as chairman of the college's board of trustees
and pastor of the church to which the paper's editor belonged. The
criticisms continued on all sides, but many persons continued their
friendship and support for Luther Rice.

Following the convention, some of those who were interested
in saving the college met with Rice in New York to discuss the
desperate situation. They figured that a minimum of $50,000 was
needed, or all would be lost. At the same time they realized that
donors would be reluctant to contribute to a dying cause. Directors
of the campaign were appointed for each area and agents under
them for districts in each area. This elaborate organization did not
prove to be effective.

The "friends of the college" meeting in New York had a form
printed for each donor to sign. It included a statement assuring donors that their gifts would be payable only after the full $50,000
had been subscribed and a committee of leading Baptists—whose
names were listed—certified "that the state of the financial concern
of said College warrants the payment of the money."

As usual, Rice had to do most of the work. Two weeks after the 1826 convention in New York he wrote from Richmond to Obadiah Brown, "I have got upon my books $6,400 towards the $50,000." He cautioned Brown to be sure that interest on the loan from John Quincy Adams be paid on time so that the President would be "recommending the college in his message" [to Congress].

Rice expressed in the same letter his concern lest the board of trustees become predominantly non-Baptist and "attempt some alteration of the charter by the aid of Congress next session." Since the institution was no longer under the control of the Baptist convention, there was indeed a likelihood of this sooner or later.

Faced with an apparently hopeless situation and displeased that Rice was not raising funds faster, six college trustees resigned; president Staughton and three professors resigned in the spring of 1827. The college had to close. Rice was in Caroline County, Virginia at the time, exhausted and intermittently ill with high fever.

Rice said he was sometimes asked, "How can the college be so much in debt after all that has been collected for it?" In reply he explained that the debt, then $95,000, was approximately the cost of property and buildings. The $40,000 or so received in donations had been paid out in interest on loans, expenses of agents, and the running of the institution.

Ultimate Giving

The poor man, Luther Rice, spent nothing on himself except absolute necessities in travel. He gave even his small savings and few pieces of furniture to the college. He absorbed the criticisms and even apologized to several whose attacks he had given mild response and received their "forgiveness."

"I have no private property," he wrote Brown, "while the college owes one cent. . . . Leave me and the debts yoked together." He sent this message in his resignation as college trustee, hoping this would mollify his critics:

> Let me perish if thereby the college can be saved! . . . As for myself personally, that is much the smallest portion of the concern! I have even

prayed that the Lord will take me away, if that should be needful in order to the saving of the college.

He still worried that Baptists might lose the institution. He wrote to Brown:

> Let me earnestly entreat you to see to it that you keep a sufficient number of true Baptists in the acting board and don't put in too many that are not Baptists to insure Baptists' support, we must have Baptist trustees, at least a majority in the acting board.

There was delay in securing a new president and faculty. The college remained closed for what would have been the 1827–1828 session. Stephen Chapin, recommended by Rice, accepted the presidency in June 1828, and two of the previous instructors returned.

Rice was making good progress, mostly in the South, toward the securing of pledges for the $50,000 needed to save the college. Debts were still such a burden, however, that he feared arrest in connection with unmet obligations. He wrote to Brown:

> I expect, if the Lord wills, to be at Washington the tenth on my way to Kentucky. Whether there is now danger from the marshal or constables, I don't know, but I think you had better not mention the fact of my intended visit there to anyone.

In May 1829 Rice forwarded to the college's board of trustees the funds he had collected. He wrote:

> Toiling as I have done for the Institution without any compensation and even providing for my personal expenses of late by special means, I am without home and utterly destitute of property. However, after having labored for the benefit of this college nearly ten years it is a source of no small consolation to me that it has now the prospect of realizing complete relief, ultimate enlargement.

Seeking still to calm the critics, he sent in this report to the board of trustees his resignation as its agent. He continued after that, as he always had, to give every ounce of his energy to the raising of the needed support.

In the midst of rejection, loss of reputation, poverty, occasional ill health, and arduous travel, Rice could still dream. In 1830 he wrote to Brown that he hoped to get an appointment as postmaster for College Hill in Washington. This would evidently provide free franking for his voluminous correspondence. He said he would live in a room there and

> make frequent excursions in different directions to collect college funds: *First*, to pay off the debts . . . *second*, to raise $15,000 for the permanent support of an instructor . . . and *third*, to raise scholarships of $2,000 each for the support of young ministers. . . . If I should live long enough to raise the fund . . . I should think that my life had not been spent in vain.

Rice was even dreaming again of getting married. He courted a wealthy widow, "Mrs. G.," still planning to establish his home at the college. As in the case of Rebecca Eaton, however, these plans came to nothing. It was suggested that Mrs. G. might have feared that her wealth would be poured into the college's slough of financial despondency.

Rice continued his travels. He had not attended the previous Triennial Convention, but in 1831 he went to the one in New York. Reports of expansion in mission fields were encouraging; seventy-two foreign missionaries were being supported.

Rice's speeches in Kentucky on Baptists' need for good educational institutions resulted in the establishment of Georgetown College. He was asked to become its president but declined.

While in Providence, Rhode Island, Rice suffered a mild stroke. Asked if he were prepared to die, he replied, "Yes, though I should like to bring up the college first." He referred of course to Columbian College. In the 1830s he dreamed of settling down to a pastorate in Washington, but the financial condition of the college never reached the point where he felt he could give up his interminable travels and begging.

His last Triennial Convention was in May 1835. Delegates attended from nineteen states and reported a Baptist constituency of more than 600,000 in over 8,000 churches. There were 112 foreign missionaries, and a budget of $100,000 was adopted for the following year.

In the summer of 1836, as usual, Rice was traveling with his two-wheeled sully and faithful horse Columbus from one to another of the churches, associational meetings, state conventions, and camp meetings in Virginia and the Carolinas. Attacked by a pain in his side and nausea as he was headed for north Georgia, he turned aside to the home of a friend, Andrew Jackson Coleman, in Edgefield County, South Carolina. In this home and that of a doctor nearby, Rice languished for almost a month, growing steadily weaker with what doctors thought might be "abscess of the liver" or appendicitis. He died peacefully on 25 September 1836 and was buried nearby.

Columbian College became free of debt in 1842. Its control passed to non-Baptists in 1904, and its name was changed to George Washington University.

Alexis Caswell, Rice's successor as treasurer of Columbian College, said of him:

> It was my duty to go over the books and examine all the receipts and disbursements. He has been aspersed. He has been accused of peculation. But he was never guilty of peculation. . . .
>
> In powers of mind he was wholly unsurpassed. He was a marked man everywhere. He was beyond the charge of dishonesty. He never appropriated a dollar to his own use. He wanted simple food and raiment and gave all the rest to open channels for a preached gospel. He preached like an angel. He had great weaknesses. One was excessive hopefulness.

Luther Rice gave his life without reserve to causes he believed in and considered vitally important. His commitment was total. He qualified in many ways as practical-minded, but he never learned to whittle his dreams down to funds available. A Leading church historian, William H. Whitsitt, declared that the coming of Luther Rice to serve his denomination was "the most important event in Baptist history in the nineteenth century."

Note on Sources

The closing quotation in this sketch is from Weaver. (Used by permission.) A half dozen quotes are from Taylor. The remaining quotations, taken from Thompson's biography, derive from original sources or rather early nineteenth century publications—Rice's Journal, letters, convention minutes, *Baptist Missionary Magazine Latter Day Luminary*, etc. (Used by permission of Broadman Press.)

Selected Bibliography

Carleton, William A. *The Dreamer Cometh*. Atlanta: Home Mission Board, SBC, 1960.

Pollard, Edward B. *Luther Rice: Pioneer in Missions and Education*. Philadelphia: Judson Press, 1928.

Taylor, James B. *Memoir of the Rev. Luther Rice, One of the First American Missionaries to the East*. Baltimore: 1840.

Thompson, Evelyn Wingo *Luther Rice: Believer in Tomorrow*. Nashville: Broadman Press, 1967.

Weaver, Rufus W. "The Place of Luther Rice in American Baptist Life." *Review and Expositor* 33 (April 1936): 121-45.

Lott Cary—
Pioneer in Liberia

Ex-slave Lott Cary and an associate were the first Americans to be appointed missionaries to Africa. Cary achieved prominence in Liberia as a pastor, educator, practical physician, and the country's acting head of state.

Lott was born about 1780 and grew up as the only child of slave parents on the William A. Christian plantation in Charles City County, about thirty miles southeast of Richmond, Virginia. His father belonged to the local Baptist church. His mother professed her faith in Christ near the end of her life. A grandmother, Mihala, exercised the strongest religious influence on little Lott. She cared for him while his parents worked in the fields.

Mihala related to the boy how their forebears had been captured in Africa and enslaved and transported under horrible conditions to America, there to be sold to taskmasters in many cases much harsher than Mr. Christian. She told Lott about how their distant relatives in Africa knew only idols and not the true God. Lott reportedly asked if these people thought God lived somewhere far away and did not love them; perhaps he was thinking about America, where people knew about God. The old lady answered as best she could.

She confessed a secret dream she had held in her heart. She had longed to go back to Africa and tell the people about the love of God. She knew she could not do this, but she hoped that Lott would do so when he grew up and that other messengers would follow. She promised her prayers to this end.

Preparation for Service

As a teenager and young man, Lott joined his parents and other slaves in the fields. He won the confidence of his master, who decided to give him a chance to earn his freedom. When Lott was about twenty-three years of age, William Christian allowed him to go to Richmond and find a job—unusual generosity on the part of a slaveholder—and Lott determined to make the most of the opportunity.

He obtained work as a common laborer in the Schockoe tobacco warehouse, the largest in Richmond, and began to save some of his money. Too much of the money, however—after payment for room and board—he spent on strong drink, and sometimes he became drunk. He used profane language habitually.

In 1807 at this critical juncture in his life, Lott went to church. He sat in the gallery, as was required of blacks, at Richmond's First Baptist Church. Pastor John Courtney, taking his text from John 3, preached on Nicodemus and the way of salvation. The message pierced Lott's heart. Under conviction for his waywardness, he asked God to forgive and save him. As long as he lived, he looked back on this as his salvation experience. Soon he received baptism and became a member of First Baptist Church.

Lott married during this period. Two children were born to the couple. Mrs. Cary, whose first name is unknown, soon died. By 1813 Cary had saved $850, and with it he bought freedom for himself and his children. About two years afterward, he married again.

A lay leader in First Baptist Church, William Crane, opened a night school in an old church building in Richmond. It met three evenings a week, and fifteen or twenty blacks enrolled. Crane and two assistants taught reading, writing and arithmetic. Crane often read selections from the Bible, modern literature, or the newspaper to the students. Cary's first goal was to learn to read the account of Nicodemus in John 3, which had led to his conversion; this he soon achieved. Some young men working in the warehouse helped him in his efforts to learn. He kept a book at hand for every spare moment. When Cary had made some progress in his educational program, one of the workers picked up a book the eager black student had left for a few moments and found it to be Adam Smith's *An Inquiry into the Nature and Causes of the Wealth of Nations*.

Cary's warehouse work improved so much that he was soon promoted to foreman over all the common laborers, with appropriate increase in wages. He had charge of receiving, marking, and shipping all the large casks of tobacco. He kept up with everything efficiently. A co-worker reported:

For this correctness and fidelity he was highly esteemed and frequently rewarded by the owner with a five-dollar note. He was allowed, also, to sell for his own benefit, many small parcels of waste tobacco.

In addition, he engaged in some brokerage business on his own, thus adding to his income. His savings reached $1,500, and with this amount he bought a house and some land just south of Richmond. He moved his little family there.

Cary felt the call to preach, and First Baptist Church of Richmond licensed him. He held services among the black people of Richmond, who were finally allowed to organize their own church with Cary as pastor. In the times he could be free from his daily work, he traveled outside the city to preach to blacks in towns as far east as Norfolk and as far west as Lynchburg. They listened with appreciation to his messages, and groups of believers grew. Collin Teague, a freed slave and a Baptist, worked closely with Cary in church activities. Teague said he considered Lott Cary the finest preacher he was in the habit of hearing. He stated openly to white ministers that he didn't hear any of them that could preach like Lott Cary.

A prominent Presbyterian minister later testified of Cary:

A sermon that I heard from Mr. Cary . . . was the best extemporaneous sermon I ever heard. It contained more original and impressive thoughts, some of which are distinct in my memory [years after Cary's death] and can never be forgotten.

William Crane, Cary's teacher, had a profound conviction of the need for mission work at home and abroad. A son born to the Cranes received the name William Carey in honor of the great pioneer missionary to India. Crane read to the students in his school from mission reports and other such materials. He informed them about the organization of Baptists nationwide in 1814 as the General Missionary Convention and the establishment of the American Colonization Society two and one-half years later.

The purpose of the latter organization was to offer a partial solution to the slavery problem by settling freed slaves in Africa. Among the founders and supporters of this movement were prominent pastors and men in public life such as Henry Clay, Francis

Scott Key, and President James Monroe. Many persons, including some blacks, opposed it as inadequate and demeaning. The society, in cooperation with the U. S. government, sent its representatives to the west African coast in 1818 to find suitable sites for colonization and make arrangements for settlements.

News of these developments apparently made little impression on other students in Crane's evening school, but it excited the mind of Lott Cary and pricked his heart in missionary challenge. He began to impress upon members of his church the need to take the gospel to the lands from which their ancestors had come. Gladdened by enthusiastic response, he led in organizing among blacks of the area the Richmond African Missionary Society, an auxiliary to the General Missionary Convention and intended for the promotion of missions in Africa. It sent contributions each year to the mission board of the Triennial Convention.

Colonial Mission Appointees

The Richmond city fathers always showed reluctance to permit black organizations unless they were led by whites. The mission society therefore elected William Crane as president and corresponding secretary. He represented this society at the Baptist national convention for twenty years. When the Southern Baptist Convention was organized, he was the chief advocate of African missions.

At the second meeting of the national group, the Triennial Convention, Crane urged—in the name of the black society in Richmond—a mission to Africa. The idea received official sanction at this meeting. At the following meeting in 1820, its mission board agreed to cooperate with the Richmond society and appointed Lott Cary and Collin Teague as missionaries to Africa.

The Colonization Society decided on the coastlands of western equatorial Africa as offering most favorable circumstances for settlements, and it recruited freed blacks in the United States to establish them. It appointed agents—all of them white persons—to carry out negotiations for available territory. The U. S. government cooperated, appointing agents of its own and chartering ships for transport.

The first of these ships seems to have been the *Elizabeth*, which sailed for Africa in February 1820. Its eighty-eight colonists were settled temporarily on the small island of Sherbro, off the coast of Sierra Leone. The entire area was administered by Great Britain as a refuge for freed slaves. Within a few weeks twenty of the American colonists had died of tropical diseases, as had all the agents.

Undeterred by reports of these dire events, Cary and Teague joined the colonization project later that same year. Led by newly-appointed agents of government and of the Colonial Society, they were to sail on the chartered ship *Nautilus*. When Cary's employers at the tobacco warehouse learned that he purposed to transfer his religious service from Virginia to Africa, they offered to raise his annual wages from $800 to $1,000 if he would remain. With polite thanks, he refused.

After various people had tried to dissuade him from his purpose, he declared: "I wish to go to a country where I shall be estimated by my merits, not complexion; and I feel bound to labor for my suffering race."

He preached a farewell sermon at First Baptist Church of Richmond, using Romans 8:32 as his text: "He that spared not his own Son, but delivered him up for us all how shall he not with him also freely give us all things?" At the close of his message he said:

> I am about to leave you and expect to see your faces no more. I long to preach to the poor Africans the way of life and salvation. I don't know what may befall me, whether I may find a grave in the ocean, or among the savage men, or . . . of wild beasts . . ., nor am I anxious about what may become of me. I feel it my duty to go.

Cary and Teague received a letter of instructions from William Staughton, corresponding secretary of the board of managers for missions in the Triennial Convention. (He had as a youth joined with William Carey and a few others in the establishment of the Baptist Missionary Society in England.) The letter stated:

> Members of the board possess a deep anxiety for your preservation, in a country where so many colonists have recently found a grave. . . . Adopt the most prudent measures for the health and safety of yourselves and families. . . . Instill the sacred truths of the gospel with meekness

and wisdom. . . . Dwell much on the doctrine of the cross . . ., the power
of God.

The mission board of the Triennial Convention gave $100 for
Cary and Teague to buy books and $200 for other expenses. The
Richmond society regarded the two men as its missionaries and
paid much of the $700 in passage costs. Cary personally defrayed
a considerable part of passage and outfit expenses for his family.

Just before departure from Richmond, Cary, Teague, and
another colonist—along with their wives and Teague's son, Hilary
—gathered in the home of deacon William Crane and organized
themselves into a Baptist church with Lott Cary as pastor.

Seeking a Homeland

As the group of colonists prepared to board the *Nautilus*, Cary declared to those around him that the step he was about to take was
not for his own advancement, for he had sacrificed all of his
worldly possessions in the venture, nor was it the result of sudden
impulse or feeling. He had counted the cost and was ready to en-
dure whatever lay ahead, even death itself, in order to witness to
his brothers in Africa and serve their needs for Christ's sake.

The ship sailed from Norfolk early on the morning of 23 January 1821 with twenty-eight colonists and their children on board,
as well as government and Colonization Society agents. The voyage took forty-four days. The ship docked at Freetown, Sierra
Leone. Many of the 1,200 ex-slaves who already lived in the area
were Americans who had escaped or whose fathers (or grand-
fathers) had served with the British in the American Revolution.

Agents of the Colonial Society and the government arranged
for the newly-arrived American colonists, along with survivors
from Sherbro Island, to settle temporarily at Fourah Bay near Freetown, where they worked on a large plantation. Agents tried with
little success to negotiate with native chieftains to obtain colonizing
land farther down the coast. The government agents gave priority
to finding places for recently enslaved natives who perforce had
been freed by U.S. agents and Navy ship captains.

Cary declared in a letter to mission secretary Staughton that he deplored the Triennial Convention's decision to link its mission with the project of the Colonial Society because the society was motivated primarily by political and humanitarian considerations, very little—if at all—by concern for Christian missions.

Cary himself never forgot his missionary purpose. He wrote to Staughton:

> I believe that just over on the Bullom side [beyond Freetown] is a beautiful field for missionary labors, among the Mandingoes. . . . They have acquired some knowledge of the English language . . . and as they are dependent on this place for trade, any traveler or any settler among them would be perfectly safe . . ., as they fear that the injuring of the missionary or settler would have a tendency to interrupt their trade with this place. . . . If you intend doing any thing for Africa, you must not wait for the Colonization Society, nor for government, for neither of these are in search of missionary ground, but of colonizing grounds; if missionary seeds [are not sown], you cannot expect a missionary crop.

The health of Lott Cary's wife, who had been unwell before departure from America's shores, worsened under the primitive conditions of life in Africa. Convinced that she was going to die, she called her husband to her side and told him so. "I am not afraid to trust my Master," she said. "I am not afraid to die."

Cary said to her:

> The few years we have been together have been spent in love and peace, and now I am about to sustain the greatest loss I can sustain in this world, except my own soul. Yet . . . seeing the afflictions that you have already gone through, and believing you will be freed from them all, I freely give you up into the hands of your best beloved.

Alone on distant and perilous shores, Cary was left to care for his three children.

He continued to preach among the colonists and Mandingoes. Cary alternated with Elijah Johnson, a freed slave from New York, in conducting worship services for the colonists each Sunday, and they cooperated in conducting an inter-denominational Sunday school.

A Beachhead Established

Late in 1821 the Colonization society appointed a physician, Dr. Eli Ayers, as chief agent, who gave vigorous leadership. In Freetown he enlisted the assistance of Captain Robert Stockton of the U.S. schooner *Alligator*, and they sailed about 250 miles down the coast to Cape Montserado (or Mesurado). Previous agents had received fairly encouraging response from Bassa chieftains regarding the settlement of colonists in that area. The native rulers would not agree, however, to give up their lucrative part in the slave trade.

Ayers and Stockton secured the services of a mulatto trader, John Mills, to translate and begin negotiations with "King Peter" and other Bassa chiefs. The latter would commit themselves to nothing definite and prolonged discussions endlessly. Stockton hurried up negotiations by pointing a loaded pistol at the main chief's head. This show of force persuaded King Peter to put his mark to a treaty ceding in perpetuity an ill-defined tract of land that would eventually become Liberia.

As payment for the land, the chiefs received a large number of items—some to be handed over at the time of the agreement and some to come later. The list included six muskets, twelve other guns, three barrels of gun powder, two boxes of beads, a keg of nails, two hogheads of tobacco, a barrel of rum, ten iron pots, a dozen spoons, six pieces of cloth, four hats, three coats, three pairs of shoes, three handkerchiefs, four umbrellas, a box of soap, twenty mirrors, and on and on.

In the early part of 1822, Ayers made several trips to bring the American colonists from Sierra Leone. Cary and Teague and their families were among the group, but Teague soon returned with his family to Sierra Leone and remained there for years. About eighty colonists resided in hastily built native style huts under very primitive conditions on Perseverance Island at the mouth of the Montserado River.

Seeing little future for themselves on this low-lying bit of land that was scarcely more than 500 yards in length, the colonists began to move onto the mainland at Cape Montserado, which would later become Monrovia. The cape itself was thirty-six miles long and one and one-half to three miles wide. Forests and thick undergrowth covered almost all of it. The original settlement of native style huts lay about two miles from the point of the cape.

The colonists were faced with bleak prospects. Day after day the hostile aborigines glared at them from nearby woods. The rainy season had also begun. Most of the colonists decided they would be better off in Sierra Leone. The agent, who resided still on the boat that had brought the settlers, came ashore to arrange for departure of the colonists. Cary and a few others refused to go, and their courage emboldened the entire group. All of the settlers decided to stay.

A white man, Jehudi Ashmun, was the leader of one shipload of colonists from America that arrived at Cape Montserado early in August 1822. Tall and slender, of fair complexion and unhealthy in appearance, he seemed to be a poor prospect for survival in Africa. Actually, he did not intend to remain long. He went on the expedition, accompanied by his wife, as a representative of the Colonial Society primarily to transport the blacks and get them settled. He hoped for quick profits in trade to pay large debts previously incurred in the U.S.

Twenty-eight years of age at the time, Ashmun had grown up a Congregationalist and as a youth expressed hope of becoming a missionary. He received a classical university education and served for a time as an unordained worker in the Episcopal church. The challenge of an almost hopeless situation in Montserado, however, grew on Ashmun. As an appendage to his instructions, the Colonization Society had authorized him to take overall responsibility in the absence of an appointed agent of the society.

The natives were obviously grouping for attack, and the colonists organized themselves for survival. Elijah Johnson was the only man among them with military experience. (He had served as an artilleryman in the War of 1812.) Wishing to give his full time to measures for defense, he suggested that Jehudi Ashmun take charge of government.

Ashmun issued a proclamation that ranks as the first document of state in Liberian history. It declared the settlement to be under military law, with Elijah Johnson in charge of defense. Although there may have been as many as 130 colonists, only thirty-five or fewer men were capable of bearing arms. They were assisted by about half a dozen men who had been recently freed from slavery in the area and three or four friendly tribesmen.

The proclamation named a captain for each of the small cannon that settlers had at their disposal and listed men under the command of each. The most effective cannon, a brass-mounted swivel fieldpiece, would occupy a position near the center of the settlement where a small masonry tower had been built, with other cannons at the corners of the clearing. According to the proclamation, every man should keep his musket with him always, whether at work or on duty at a cannon. Armed men would be on guard at all times. No useless firing would be permitted, and in case of alarm every man should rush to his post and do his duty.

In the proclamation Lott Carey was named as health officer. In this capacity he began to educate himself in medicine, as best he could under the circumstances. From then until the end of his days he did the work of a physician in the colony at no charge to his patients. He specialized in tropical diseases of the area, of which Mrs. Ashmun and many colonists died.

The Struggle for Survival

The settlers knew that their lives and the existence of the colony were immediately at stake. Tribal war drums sounded ominously in the distance. The treaty the chiefs had felt forced to sign meant nothing to them. King Peter assembled an army of 800 warriors and determined to annihilate the American settlement. The attack came at dawn on 11 November 1822.

A band of enemy warriors emerged from the jungle sixty yards away. They fired their muskets then ran forward ten abreast, screaming and brandishing their spears menacingly. They overran the western gun emplacement before the colonists had a chance to fire the cannon, then headed toward the masonry tower.

If King Peter's forces had immediately charged this tower, to which gunners from the western emplacement had fled, they could have easily overrun the settlement and destroyed the colony. Some of the native warriors were diverted, however, by the lure of plunder in the huts they were passing on the western side. This put the enemy attack in disarray and gave Ashmun, Johnson, and Cary time to rally the confused colonial defenders, who fired their remaining cannon with ball and grapeshot into the ranks of the tribesmen, forcing the attackers into retreat. They could do no more than collect their dead and wounded and flee into the jungle.

Of the colonists, two children and a woman were killed, and two women were seriously wounded. The enemy loss in dead and wounded was estimated between 100 and 150. Ashmun commended his little band of fighting men for their bravery. He cited Lott Cary particularly for his courage and combat skills.

The colonists had to keep up and intensify defensive measures. Renewed attack could be expected at any time. Earthwork fortifications were strengthened and enlarged. Men stood on guard around the clock, and others could be mobilized at a moment's notice. In one of his letters Cary compared the situation to that of the Jews who "grasped a weapon in one hand, while they labored with the other" (Jer 4:17). Then he added, "There never has been an hour or a minute, no, not even when the balls were flying round my head, when I could wish myself again in America."

King Peter assembled a larger force—perhaps about 1,500 warriors—that struck in the early morning of 1 December, attacking from two sides. The colonists drove them back. Ten minutes later the enemy surged forward again, fighting harder and suffering many casualties. A third attempt had the same result. Two cannons opened fire on the invaders, and they retreated. The attacking force tried again—and still another time. The natives were handicapped by their inexperience with artillery. They required half an hour to load and fire the guns each time, a task that the Americans accomplished four to six times a minute. Despite these odds, one settler was killed and two seriously injured.

There were further attacks in the years to come, but the existence of the colony was never again seriously threatened by military force. The natives became convinced of the white man's invincibility—and Africans referred to "civilized" people of any color as "white men." The colonists continued reasonable security measures and further strengthened fortifications but devoted more time to clearing the land and cultivating it and constructing more decent homes and government buildings. The land was fertile, the rainfall was adequate, the climate was warm, and the harvests were abundant. Rice, corn, yams, cassava plants, plantains (like bananas), pineapples, melons, sugar cane, and dozens of other products flourished.

Through fair trade with the natives, under Ashmun's lead, colonists won their confidence. By honest purchase they added to the territory under their control.

Manifold Problems

A serious disagreement developed between Ashmun and Cary, with some of the original colonists joining Cary's side. The agent who had come with the earliest settlers from Sierra Leone had at that time assigned generous lots on Cape Montserado to them. After many other colonists arrived, Ashmun perceived the need for redistributing the available space. Naturally, this did not please the original settlers. They had largely cleared and partly cultivated their land and did not want to give parts of it to newcomers.

Cary and other original settlers said they would appeal their case to the board of the Colonization Society. Until a reply could be received from the Society, they refused to work on any of the land or perform their assigned labors in public improvements.

Ashmun published an announcement on 13 December 1823 that more than a dozen able-bodied persons in the colony refused to do the work required of them. He ordered that they should receive nothing more from the public storehouse of supplies until they resumed working.

The next morning several of the earliest colonists appeared at the agency house and demanded that Ashmun rescind the order. He refused in the name of fairness and government authority. Some of the protestors then marched to the storehouse where weekly rations were being issued, seized provisions for themselves (in violation of Ashmun's order), and carried them to their homes.

Later the same day the agent issued a circular letter to the colonists declaring that the unwarrantable act of the morning would be reported to the board of the Colonization Society. He made mention particularly of Lott Cary as leader of the dissidents.

In his letter to the board relating the affair, however, Ashmun went out of his way to emphasize Cary's past record of reliability and great services to the community and to Ashmun personally. He urged, in the society's judgment of the affair, "the most indulgent construction that it will bear." In reference to his own benefit from Cary's work as physician, he wrote,

> The hand that records the lawless transaction would long since have been cold in the grave had it not been for the unwearied and painful attentions of this individual, rendered at all hours, of every description, and continued for several months.

Cary had thought he was giving needed leadership to a just cause in protesting the land redistribution. On reviewing the events in his mind, he became deeply troubled and decided that he had acted wrongly. He feared also that he had, by resisting the rightful authority of one who had reposed confidence in him, inflicted a blot on his own character and influence that could never he removed in this world.

He openly confessed his mistake to Ashmun and to the others. Feeling unworthy of continued aid, he declared his wish to receive no more of the free supplies from the community storehouse. To supplement the twelve or thirteen dollars a month he received rather regularly from the Richmond African Missionary Society, which was apparently all that was received from the U.S., he promised to support his family by his own efforts. He told Ashmun he desired to withdraw from any activities that would detract from his spiritual ministry. At the same time, he stated his readiness "to be useful in the way the agent thought fit to propose."

Ashmun suggested that Cary take the responsibility of caring for liberated Africans, helping them to return to their own tribes—if this could be arranged—or settling them into the Montserado community. Cary immediately accepted this position.

Hampered by U.S. policy that forbade interference with slave traders of nationalities other than American, Ashmun and his administration fought slavery with every means in their power. Sometimes, in one way or another—including the threat of force—enslaved persons could be freed. On one occasion, Ashmun bought 116 slaves for ten dollars each and freed them. Doubtless there were many other "hush" deals.

Making the task so difficult was the engagement of powerful chieftains in the slave trade—King Boatswain, for example, the colonists' strongest supporter and friend! A French slave trader had given him a large quantity of goods with the understanding that the king would deliver to the slaver on the latter's next visit a considerable number of young slaves. The Frenchman, who was always punctual, was due soon to return, and Boatswain did not have the slaves for him.

The chief looked around to locate peaceful tribes that might be easy victims. He decided on the Queahs, a small agricultural and trading people of the most inoffensive character. He sent his warriors to the various Queah hamlets, and they attacked simultaneously in the middle of the night. The Queahs made no resistance. Most of their villages were totally destroyed, with every hut burned and every man, woman, and small child murdered. The boys and girls, likely younger teenagers, were taken captive to fulfill the contract with the French slaver.

Despite such incidents, the colonists developed additional settlements farther inland, and a number of native towns were brought under colonial administration to some extent.

Cary gave much of his time to the establishment of schools for children in Cape Montserado and did much of the teaching himself. The colonial society sent some teachers at Cary's pleading, but they succumbed to the deadly climate. The schools declined; some closed because of inadequate funds and the scarcity of teachers.

The enthusiastic missionary started many Sunday schools also. He ministered regularly in Providence Baptist Church, which was the continuation of the one that had been organized in the home of Deacon Crane in Richmond. Membership reached 100, and an attractive chapel was erected. The Methodists built a church house also. Cary organized a missionary society of forty-five members in his church, modeled on the one he had established among black Baptists in Richmond. He was elected president of the society.

Faithful Services

Jehudi Ashman, who had been acting agent and governor most of the time for nearly three years, was officially named as agent by the Colonization Society in May 1825. Following this appointment, he led in the establishment of a more permanent government for the colony, its laws modeled in general on those of the United States. The Colonization Society's agent would be governor, and the settlers would elect his associate, the vice agent, and a colonial council that would enact needed laws, but these were subject to approval by the agent and ultimately by the Colonization Society. Certain offices such as sheriffs and justices of the peace could be colonists; the agent made the appointments.

These developments, including the promotion of Ashmun, came in consequence of a brief visit to Cape Montserado in the summer of 1824 by Ralph R. Gurley, special agent of the Colonization Society. He developed high admiration and appreciation for Ashmun, who had been unjustly denigrated by a former agent and largely ignored by the board of the society. Gurley praised the character and work of Lott Cary also. Evidently this special agent led the society to name the new country Liberia and its capital (Montserado) Monrovia, in honor of retiring U.S. President James Monroe.

The Colonization Society, wishing to have the support of a leading colonist to promote recruitment for the project in the United States, invited Cary to attend its meetings in the spring of 1826. As he was almost ready to embark, however, another shipload of settlers arrived—as others had come several times a year since the beginning. Of this shipload, however, a much larger number than usual fell ill immediately with tropical diseases. Cary and Ashmun agreed that Cary must remain to attend to their medical needs, hoping he would have a later opportunity to visit the United States.

A few months afterward the colonists elected Cary vice agent in the government, which increased his duties greatly. He remained in the office until his death. Gurley said of Cary:

> In his good sense, moral worth, public spirit, courage, resolution, and decision, the Colonial Agent had perfect confidence. He knew that in times of difficulty or danger, reliance might be placed upon the energy and efficiency of Mr. Cary.

Ashmun had been often and for long periods brought low by tropical diseases, as were Cary and many others. Aided by the medical care of Cary, Ashmun managed to continue vigorous administration of the government. He was firm but forbearing and patient. He delegated authority and gave officials freedom to carry out their responsibilities. He manifested absolute integrity in dealing both with the colonists and native people. He purchased and traded for territory almost half the length of Liberia's coastline today. Inland, jurisdiction remained mostly with tribal leaders.

In March 1828 Governor Ashmun fell ill once again. Cary as his physician urged him to leave the unhealthy climate and return to the U.S. to regain his health—his only hope of survival. Ashmun embarked on 26 March, confidently leaving Cary as head of government. By this time there were about 1,200 settlers in the colony. Ashmun left detailed instructions or suggestions for every aspect of the administration.

Ashmun came near death more than once during the voyage, and he had to spend several weeks on an inland in the West Indies trying to regain some strength. He survived the voyage and proceeded to New Haven, Connecticut, where he died on 25 August at the age of thirty-four soon after being taken ashore. On his deathbed he urged that Lott Cary be made permanent agent and governor in Liberia. Ralph R. Gurley, secretary-general of the Colonization Society, attended Ashmun in his last hours, and he heartily approved the suggestion.

Meanwhile, Cary efficiently administered affairs in the colony —restructuring the jail, refurbishing the government house, completing a housing project on public farms, celebrating 4 July impressively, opening additional roads, locating new settlers to their lands, and strengthening the colony's defenses.

Bassa tribesmen broke into the storehouse at a Liberian trading center in Digby, a few miles north of Monrovia, and stole its valuable contents. They then turned over use of the building to a slave dealer. Cary sent a letter to the slave dealer demanding that he evacuate the colonists' building immediately. He also sent three emissaries—including Elijah Johnson—to King Bristol (or Brister) of the Bassas, demanding satisfaction. Cary's letter was intercepted by natives and destroyed. The king imprisoned the Liberian emissaries, instead of paying damages and punishing those guilty of the offenses. Cary immediately organized a volunteer relief force to rescue them.

On the evening of 8 November 1828, Cary and seven other men busied themselves in the old agency house of Monrovia, making cartridges to supply the rescue force. A tragic accident occurred. Apparently a burning candle was inadvertently upset, and it ignited some loose powder all the way to kegs of ammunition. The resulting explosion blew up the structure. All eight volunteer workers suffered mortal injury: Six died the next day; Cary and one other survived a day longer.

James B. Taylor, later the first corresponding secretary of the Foreign Mission Board of the Southern Baptist Convention, declared:

> Lott Cary was among the most gifted men of the present age. Appropriately it was remarked that "he was one of nature's noblemen." Under more favorable circumstances, he would have been on a level with the most intellectual and honored of his race. . . .

> He possessed a mind of no ordinary grade. . . . This was evidenced from the period of his employment at the warehouse in Richmond to his elevation as presiding officer in the colony of Liberia. There was a clearness and vigor of thought enabling him to combine and compare ideas and to reach with ease the best and most rational conclusion.

Further, Taylor wrote of Cary's abilities as a speaker and his "unbending integrity," adding that "He aimed most conscientiously to discharge his duty, whatever might be the consequences."

Note on Sources

Fitts' brief biography of Cary was quite useful in the preparation of the present sketch. Two of the quotations come uniquely from Ralph Gurley's work. Six quotations are from J. B. Taylor. Five additional quotations are in both Gurley's and Taylor's works.

Selected Bibliography

Fitts, Leroy. *Lott Carey: First Black Missionary to Africa*. Valley Forge PA: Judson Press, 1978.
Gurley, Ralph R. "Sketch of the Life of the Rev. Lott Cary." In *Life of Jehudi Ashmun, Late Colonial Agent in Liberia*. New York, 1835.
Taylor, James B. "Lott Cary." In *Virginia Baptist Ministers*. (1837): 396-444.

Editor's Note

Lott Cary preferred this spelling of his name rather than the traditional one, "Carey," that is used in most references to him.

William Knibb—
Missionary and Liberator

As a schoolboy, Will Knibb distinguished himself as a marble play-
er, but he was rather ordinary in his studies. Strongly built and
unafraid, he was quick to take an active part in defending a weaker child against one or more bullies. The disposition to help the
disadvantaged, even when it endangered himself, remained with
him all of his days.

Will had a twin sister, two other sisters, and three brothers.
Will's father was a tailor who failed at his trade and manifested no
religious faith. His mother was a Christian believer and tried to see
that the children attended Sunday School in a Congregational
church. Will was taken from school at the age of twelve and apprenticed to a printer. His brother Thomas, four years older, had
followed the same course earlier.

As a teenager working in a print shop in Bristol, England, William received baptism and joined the Broadmead Baptist Church.
Dr. John Ryland, pastor of the church, was principal of Bristol College, the oldest Baptist theological school, and also served on the
executive committee of the Baptist Mission Society. Andrew Fuller,
recently deceased, had been chairman of this committee, and his
son owned the print shop in which William worked. Reports of the
mission society were printed there, and the youth began to read
about mission work. He also taught a Sunday School class and did
some preaching in poverty-stricken sections of the city

Missionary Teaching and More

Thomas Knibb received appointment by the mission society. He
served as a teacher and preacher in Jamaica but died of tropical
fever fifteen months after arrival there. William Knibb had already
indicated his desire for missionary service, but leaders of the mission society regarded him as much less gifted than Thomas. He
was considered for Sumatra, but Ryland doubted that he would be
able to learn a foreign language. William tried to make up his

deficiency in formal education by studying Samuel Johnson's dictionary during mealtimes at the print shop.

When news came of Thomas's death, William said, "If the society will accept me, I'll go and take his place." Unwilling to appoint him as a minister for Jamaican churches, the society assigned him to the West Indian island as a teacher for mission schools. He took a three-month course with the British and Foreign School Society, married, and left with his wife Mary for Jamaica. They arrived in Kingston, the chief city, early in 1825. William was twenty-one years of age, and his wife was five years older.

Jamaica, 145 miles long and 50 miles wide at its broadest point, was noted for its scenery and lush vegetation, despite storms and sometimes drought. Various tropical diseases threatened foreigners especially. The economy depended on sugar production from the cane crops, mostly on large plantations. Absentee Britishers owned these as a rule and others of the same nationality supervised them. A privileged black slave, the "driver," kept a small group of slaves at work and administered discipline. He carried a long leather cartwhip that could lacerate the flesh.

Jamaica had a legislative assembly of 47 members elected by about 2,200 voters—white landowners and a few "colored" (those of mixed blood). The assembly passed harsh legislation to keep the 30,000 slaves in total subjection. Some of these measures were so extreme that the government in London disallowed them. The British government kept check through a governor in Jamaica.

The Anglican Church was officially established in Jamaica and supported by general taxation. Very few of the members attended services. There were eight Baptist churches with a total membership of about 5,000—most of them slaves—with smaller numbers of Methodists, Presbyterians, Moravians, and Catholics. The "sectarian" churches were barely tolerated. Baptist preachers, the missionaries, were most hated by the planters because several of them expressed sympathy for the black slaves, who were whipped mercilessly and mistreated in many other ways.

At the time of Knibb's appointment, "instructions" from the mission society's committee referred to the conditions of Negro slavery that he would find in Jamaica as exclusively a political matter. The instructions warned:

You must ever bear in mind that as a resident of Jamaica, you have nothing whatever to do with its civil or political affairs, and with these you must never interfere.

When he arrived in Jamaica, Knibb was assigned to teach black children and perhaps a few colored children in the same school that his brother Thomas had served. Soon he was traveling each Sunday by canoe to preach at Port Royal, near Kingston, where his brother also had proclaimed the gospel. William did not have the license required by Jamaican authorities for preaching. For this he needed a recommendation from the Baptist Missionary Society, which it was reluctant to give. Finally the society did so, and after further delays Knibb received the license.

Breaking Point for the Oppressed

Knibb resigned his teaching position in 1829 and went to Savanna-la-Mar in the Southwestern part of the island to start a mission church. There he had his first encounter with the authorities over treatment of a slave. The missionary had been ill but improved enough to fill a preaching appointment in Falmouth, on the North-western coast. Sam Swiney, a deacon in the Savanna-la-Mar church, went with a few others to Knibb's house on an Easter Sunday evening to conduct a prayer service. They prayed for their pastor's full recovery and safe return. Sam Swiney was arrested and charged with breaking the law, and others of the group were also detained because the Jamaican assembly had previously enacted legislation forbidding any slave to teach or preach without official permission.

Knibb received word of the trouble and rushed back to Savanna-la-Mar. He gathered witnesses for the defense, but the magistrate who was trying the case paid little attention to their testimony. He said that Swiney's praying "from his head" without a prayer book before him was the same as preaching. Knibb spoke out so insistently on his deacon's rights that the magistrate threatened to take away his license to preach if he did not keep quiet. Swiney was convicted of "preaching and teaching." His sentence included twenty lashes on the bare back and two weeks at hard labor. Other worshipers who had been detained were released.

Knibb went to the flogging the next morning. Swiney was "stretched indecently on the ground, held firmly down by four slaves, two at his hands and two at his feet," Knibb wrote his mission society. The driver ordered to administer this punishment was "merciful," Knibb continued the account, "or every lash would have fetched blood."

Immediately after the whipping, Swiney was chained to another convict and sent to work, probably on the roads outside of the town. Knibb walked by his side, which angered the supervisors. He took Swiney's hand and promised, loudly enough for all around to hear, to do everything he could to help him. Knibb's report to the society was forwarded to the Colonial Office in London, which contributed eventually to the dismissal of the governor in Jamaica.

Knibb accepted a call to become pastor of the Baptist church in Falmouth. The town claimed a population of 2500; and the church numbered about 700 members, mostly slaves. Knibb moved his wife and three daughters and a son there, and he remained in this pastorate as long as he lived.

Anti-slavery forces were active in Britain. Many Jamaican slaves learned of this and became convinced that the king had granted freedom, which the planters were withholding from them. Knibb and other pastors assured them this was not the case, but some slaves continued to believe the rumors. Late in 1831, Sam Sharp, a domestic slave and a deacon in the Baptist church of Montego Bay, about twenty miles from Falmouth, gathered a group of those slaves who were determined to claim their rights.

The group planned a strike. They would spread the word among other slaves and refuse to go back to work after the Christmas holidays unless they were paid wages. Knibb heard of the plan and pled with the slaves not to execute it. He threatened them with the loss of his friendship and the wrath of God if they did not give up this hopeless effort, based on false rumor of freedom, and return to work after the holidays. Sharp, regarded as the leader, evidently still believed that the king in England had proclaimed the slaves' freedom. He said to his followers that there should be no violence or rebellion.

Just after Christmas, when the overseers tried to force slaves to work, something like a rebellion broke out at various points in the western part of the island. Slaves stole firearms and horses and rode from one area to another to rally support, and angry slaves set fire to the properties of some planters. The Jamaican militia was called out, and it took awful vengeance. Knibb and three other Baptist pastors were summoned to the courthouse in Falmouth where they were told that they must enlist for militia duty—despite a Jamaican ordinance that ministers were exempt from such service.

Knibb reported on 3 January for militia duty as ordered. He and two other Baptist ministers were taken under armed guard to the Montego Bay courthouse, where militiamen with fixed bayonets guarded them that night. One of the cursing militiamen told Knibb he was to be shot at ten o'clock the next morning. Nothing of the kind came to pass, however, and a civil officer who was concerned for justice got the ministers released.

By this time some interior areas in the western part of the island were held by the militant slaves. Within two or three weeks the back of the insurrection was broken. Fourteen free persons had lost their lives, including four or five whites killed in active service with the militia. About 400 blacks were killed, a fourth of which were captives who were shot or hanged. At least that many more suffered the most severe floggings. Fifty houses and sugarworks had been burned, but none of this kind of violence took place on the estates where members of Knibb's church worked.

Court martials were set up all over the western part of the island for trying leaders of the insurrection. The civil courts took over after martial law came to an end on 5 February. The total number officially brought to trial was 634. Of these, 310 were sentenced to death; 285 were sentenced to prison terms, hard labor, and floggings of up to 500 lashes. Some persons died from the floggings. Only three of those persons sentenced came from Knibb's church of 980 members, and these for minor offenses such as giving food to insurrectionists. Several Baptist slaves were rewarded for protecting the property of their masters.

The last of the judicial executions was that of Sam Sharp on 23 May 1832. Sharp was a man of peace and wanted only a non-violent strike for wages.

In further vengeance the whites, supported by some colored persons, burned or otherwise destroyed Baptist church buildings and a few of those belonging to the Methodists. Militia had occupied Knibb's church in Falmouth during the time of martial law, and when they were dismissed from duty they demolished the church and its furnishings. The planters determined to destroy evangelical work and organized themselves into a society for the purpose. They had representatives in Britain spreading false reports about mission work in Jamaica. Knibb wrote to his mother about this time, shortly before her death, that he was "not safe from assassination."

Appeal to the British

The fifteen Baptist Missionaries (wives were not counted as missionaries then) decided that someone must return to the homeland and explain the true situation to mission supporters. They chose Knibb, who sailed with his family in April 1832.

At the end of the voyage as the pilot went aboard to guide the ship into port at Liverpool, Knibb asked him, "Well, pilot, what news?"

He replied, "The Reform Bill has passed." (The Reform Bill broadened representation of the people in Parliament, to which more abolitionists could be elected.)

Knibb murmured feelingly, "Thank God." As the pilot went about his business, Knibb said (most likely to his wife), "Now I'll have slavery down. I will never rest, day or night, till I see it destroyed, root and branch."

He did not know what to expect from the mission committee. From what he had heard, its members seemed to be prepared to take to task any missionary who became involved in political controversy. Knibb had private conversations with members of the committee a few days before their meeting. From only one person with whom he spoke did he receive encouragement in his stand against slavery. Mission committee chairman John Dyer advised against any strong action.

Knibb, undaunted, met with the committee. When he was recognized, he stood and said,

> Myself, my wife, and my children, are entirely dependent on the Baptist mission, we have landed without a shilling, and may at once be reduced to penury. But, if it be necessary, I will take them by the hand, and walk barefoot through the kingdom, but I will make known to the Christians of England what their brethren in Jamaica are suffering.

This fervent testimony won the committee largely to his position. The annual public meeting of the society was two days later. Knibb and another Baptist missionary from Jamaica were the principle speakers. Knibb declared in his speech that as long as the missionaries had been able to preach freely, they had kept silent about civil and political affairs. He said that unless slavery was abolished, however, the slaves would forever be denied evangelical teaching. Knibb continued, "I now stand forward as the unflinching and undaunted advocate of immediate emancipation." After this statement, applause thundered throughout the large auditorium for several minutes.

William Wilberforce and other abolitionists had been fighting for decades to get slavery abolished in the British empire. Knibb asked mission supporters to join forces with them. For more than a year he traveled about the entire country preaching and giving public lectures on slavery. Knibb was most in demand and apparently the most effective of the abolitionist speakers. Participants in the meetings testified that his face glowed as he spoke with impassioned sincerity and fervor for the cause.

The West Indian Committee of the slaveholders hired an eloquent speaker to follow Knibb as he traveled from city to city with his message in order to present their side and negate the missionary's influence. This proved quite ineffective, however. Occasionally, the two men appeared on the same program. As many as 8,000 or 9,000 admission tickets were sold to these "debates," with many persons turned away for lack of room. People in general, whenever they took part in the controversy at all, seemed strongly to support the anti-slavery position.

"I look upon the question of slavery only as one of religion and morality," Knibb declared in an address at London's Exeter Hall on 15 August 1832. "All I ask is, that my African brother may stand in the family of man; that my African sister shall, while she clasps her tender infant to her breast, be allowed to call it her own; that they both shall be allowed to bow their knees in prayer to that God who has made of one blood all nations as one flesh." At the climax of this impassioned address he held high a pair of iron slave shackles to the view of the huge audience and then threw them resoundingly to the floor, declaring that the infamy of slavery must perish from the earth.

Achievement and Celebration

Knibb, along with two Methodist missionaries, testified for several days before committees of both houses of Parliament. The evidence they gave seemed to be decisive. Representatives of the West Indian Committees brought their arguments too—that the blacks would not work if they became free, that the economy of Jamaica would be ruined, and that the evangelical missionaries were troublemakers who should be expelled from Jamaica.

The more representative reform Parliament assembled in February 1833. In stark contrast to former sessions of Parliament, reformers outnumbered conservatives four to one. Slavery had been the primary issue in the candidates' campaigns. Petitions for abolition piled up in Parliament chambers. One petition bore the signatures of 187,000 women.

After months of study, discussion, and compromise, an abolition bill passed both houses and was signed into law on 23 August 1833. It provided that slavery should be abolished in British colonies as of 1 August 1834. Owners would be remunerated to the extent of 20,000,000 pounds. Wilberforce, who was on his deathbed, thanked God that he had lived to see the day when Britain would give that huge amount for the abolition of slavery.

Knibb and another Baptist missionary (then in England) stood in danger of arrest and imprisonment for debt. After their chapels were destroyed by the planters, they had borrowed money in Jamaica to construct some kind of facilities for their large congregations. The British government, realizing that vandalism of chapels had taken place with the indulgence of its own representatives in Jamaica, appropriated 5,510 pounds to cover about half of the indebtedness—enough to free ministers from the danger of being arrested.

The mission committee had already asked Knibb to remain in Britain to raise the 17,900 pounds needed to restore the ruined Baptist chapels in Jamaica. When the job was completed, he sailed immediately with his family for Jamaica. They arrived there in late October 1834.

A tremendous crowd gathered to welcome the Knibbs. The pilot who was to guide the ship into port, a member of Knibb's church, stood all day on a hill with his telescope in order to catch sight of the incoming vessel at the earliest possible moment. Knibb later related that when they landed on the beach

> we were nearly pushed into the sea by kindness. Poor Mrs. Knibb was quite overcome. They took me up in their arms, they sang, they laughed, they wept, and I wept too.

The account also quoted the shouting slaves, "Him come, him come for true. Who da come for we king, king Knibb. Him fight de battle, him win de crown." Many of them marched in procession to the chapel grounds where a prayer service of thanksgiving was held.

For several years following nominal emancipation an "apprenticeship" system was in force. Under its vague provisions, former slave proprietors managed to keep the poor blacks in subjugation almost as before. Both men and women were beaten at the whim of their masters and placed on cruel treadmills, pursued as runaways, and denied the privilege of changing residence or work. Knibb embittered the planters against himself further by fighting the evils of this system. He believed that the ruling Jamaicans were trying to instigate another revolt in order to have a pretext for murdering more blacks.

Knibb wrote to a friend:

> I have been secretly informed that if the plan succeeds, and any riot is the result, my death is resolved on as the first that shall be sacrificed, the

abettors of slavery rightly supposing that a Baptist missionary's blood
would be the most acceptable offering to the expiring monster.

The longsuffering blacks, uniformly counseled by Knibb and
the other missionaries against violence and hatred, refused to give
the landowners any occasion for retaliation.

Pressed by British authorities and the Crown, the Jamaican
Assembly—in an effort to maintain its jurisdiction and gain some
credit—passed legislation giving all "apprentices" their full freedom, effective 1 August 1838. At the same time they sent a
protesting, almost insulting, communication to the Queen.

To celebrate freedom for the former slaves, Knibb arranged a
mass meeting in his church at Falmouth for the evening of 31 July.
Following a devotional service and just before midnight, he rose
to speak. He pointed to a large wall clock as its hands were near-
ing twelve. "The hour is at hand, the monster is dying," he
solemnly intoned. A short period of awesome silence followed, and
the clock began striking. "The monster is dead!" Knibb shouted
when the twelfth tone had reverberated through the large auditorium. "The Negro is free!" Then came a breathless moment, still and
quiet, after which the entire assembly rose and cheered for a long
time. The service closed with congregational singing.

The next day there were further meetings, with many speeches.
A large group gathered in the mission school playground, where
a grave had been dug. A slave chain, whip, and iron collar were
placed with mock solemnity in the coffin and buried as the people
sang a funeral dirge that had been composed for the occasion:
"Now, slavery, we lay thy vile form in the dust."

There were celebrations in the other chapels also. The blacks
showed commendable restraint, and the governor reported to his
superiors in London that not even a case of drunkenness was reported. The governor's report recounted also a proposal that
circulated among non-blacks to hang Knibb in effigy. "It got
abroad and magnified into a real intention of hanging that gentleman." The plan came to nothing, however.

Meeting Further Challenges

The planters were threatened with loss of the sugar monopoly for Britain, which later came to pass. Meanwhile, they strove to maintain prosperity for themselves and subjugation for the former slaves in as many ways as possible. They tried every way to make the blacks work for wages below what was required for the barest necessities of simple living. Knibb realized that some alternative must be provided for the blacks, or they could hardly survive.

He borrowed money and bought tracts of fertile land in one place after the other. He sold plots at a nominal cost to freed men who could then build cottages and cultivate the soil and raise food crops for their own families and to sell. About 20,000 former slaves took advantage of this opportunity.

Many new towns were established as a result, with a Baptist church in each one. Some of these towns were named for Queen Victoria and leaders in the emancipation movement like Wilberforce. Others bore names revealing the new hopefulness: "Try and See," "Happiness," "Harmony," "Stand Fast," "Time and Patience," and "Long-looked-for-come-at-last."

The blacks were no longer helpless pawns in the hands of planters, and the latter had to pay better wages to get workers. To keep suffrage from blacks, the Jamaican assembly raised the property qualification for voting from ten pounds to five times that amount. The planters levied fines of up to two days' wages for each day the blacks missed from work. All blacks were still taxed to support the Anglican Church.

Knibb declared in a public meeting in July 1838:

> I pledge myself, by all that is solemn and sacred never to rest satisfied, until I see my black brethren in the enjoyment of the same civil and religious liberties which I myself enjoy, and see them take a proper stand in society as men.

This struggle he waged with considerable success to the end of his life—both in Jamaica and on four trips to England—without neglect of the spiritual aspect of his missionary work.

Knibb baptized about 3,000 converts in the twenty-one years of his ministry in Jamaica. The church in Falmouth, of which he was pastor for fifteen years, grew to a membership of over 1,200. He started several other churches as well. Knibb was loved by the blacks as pastor, preacher, and friend. People came from near and far to seek his counsel for their problems. He took care to give the best guidance he could, then tried actively to help them work out their problems—especially those caused by the planters.

Knibb brought his church to full self-support in 1838. It built chapels for three of its mission stations and supported not only the pastor and an associate but seven day-school teachers and mission workers. In 1842 Knibb persuaded the other missionary pastors to relieve the mission society in Britain of its regular financial support. Members of the churches, most of whom were recently out of slavery, assumed responsibility for supporting the missionaries and their families. This plan did not prove to be easy, and the mission society helped later in some special projects, one of which was the establishment of a theological college for the training of native ministers. Knibb had promoted the idea among his fellow missionaries and in Britain. The new institution opened at Calabar in 1843 and moved to Kingston some years later. The mission society supported the college with personnel and operating funds.

For years Knibb advocated the establishment of a Jamaican Baptist mission to West Africa, from which the enslaved blacks had been brought originally. In 1839 he started a weekly paper, *Baptist Herald and Friend of Africa*. "I am confident," he wrote, "the future welfare of our churches here depends upon their imbibing a missionary spirit." He lived long enough to help actively in the sending of the first group of black missionaries to the new field in Africa.

William Knibb was a devoted husband and father, grieved by the sufferings that were brought on his family by the work to which he felt called. Four of his and Mary's nine children died in infancy. Others succumbed to tropical diseases, leaving only two daughters. Soon afterward, another son was born. One of the daughters married a missionary pastor in Jamaica. The other married a missionary also, and they served in West Africa.

Knibb could not be described as a man of profound or original powers of intellect, but he did possess good practical sense. He was an impressive public speaker, capable of arousing his hearers to action. A commanding physical appearance and a good voice helped. More important were his fearlessness and devotion to a cause in which he believed. He loved to be in the forefront of a battle for what he felt was right. He manifested deep spirituality, open-hearted friendliness, and gratitude to God for the privilege of being a missionary.

"Had I ten thousand lives," he testified, "I would spend them all in this cause." The one life he did have he spent with abandon, until that strong body succumbed to typhoid and then yellow fever. He died at the age of forty-two in November 1845, and 8,000 persons attended his funeral. One church member said afterward to the sorrowing widow, "Other ministers kind, but none can do like Massa Knibb." Mary Knibb served in Jamaica the remaining twenty years of her life.

Note on Sources

Both Payne's small book and Wright's larger one are quite well done. Quotations in this sketch come from Hinton and Landels.

Selected Bibliography

Hinton, Howard. *Memoir of William Knibb.* London, 1847.

Landels, William. "William Knibb, the Philanthropist." In *Baptist Worthies.* London, 1884.

Payne, Ernest A. *Freedom in Jamaica, Some Chapters in the Story of the Baptist Missionary Society.* London: The Carey Press, 1933.

Wright, Philip. *Knibb "the Notorious," Slaves' Missionary, 1803–1845.* London: Sidgwick and Jackson, 1973.

John Everett Clough
and the Lone Star Mission

John Everett Clough was born in the same year (1836) as the American Baptist mission to the Telegus of Southeastern India. The decision to begin the mission was made by the mission board of The Triennial Convention at its meeting in Richmond, Virginia the year before. Clough had grown up on a homesteader's farm in Iowa; from the year 1864, his life intertwined with that of the Telegu mission.

The "Lone Star"

The mission had not been very successful. The Baptist Board of Foreign Missions, an agency of the Triennial Convention, was ready several times to close it in order to apply personnel and funds to more fruitful fields. One such occasion was a meeting of the board and the convention in 1853 in Albany, New York. The mission secretary pointed to a map on the wall that indicated each mission station with a small star. He referred to the one Telegu station at Nellore as a lone star shining for Christ in that part of India.

Before he retired that evening one board member, Samuel F. Smith, scribbled some stanzas of rhyme on the back of an envelope then wrote across the top of it: "The Lone Star." The next morning as he went to breakfast, Smith showed his writing to another participant in the mission board meetings. The latter read it to the entire group at the beginning of the morning session. The effect was decisive, and the board refused to close the mission. The middle stanzas of the rhyme are:

> Shine on, "Lone Star"! in grief and tears
> And sad reverses oft baptized;
> Shine on amid thy sister spheres;
> Lone stars in heaven not despised.

Shine on, "Lone Star"! Who lifts his hand
  To dash to earth so bright a gem,
A new "lost pleiad" from the band
  That sparkles in night's diadem?

Shine on "Lone Star"! The day draws near
  When none shall shine more fair than thou;
Thou, born and nursed in doubt and fear
  Wilt glitter on Immanuel's brow.

Again in 1862 a majority favored discontinuing the Telegu work, as results were no more encouraging than before. Few converts had been won. Lyman Jewett, the missionary to the Telegus, and his wife were at home on sick leave. Jewett's doctor advised against his attending the mission board meeting but allowed it when the missionary agreed to rest quietly and not take part in deliberations. Seeing that the board was once again determined to close the Telegu mission, however, Jewett arose and declared that he intended to go back "to live and if need be die among the Telegus"—even if American Baptists would not support him.

One member of the board was reported to have said facetiously that if Brother Jewett was determined to return to his field, the least they could do was to send someone to give him a Christian funeral. In any case, at this point, the board did not vote to close the mission but decided to strengthen it.

Two years later the mission board was considering the application of John Everett Clough. The board was not in general disposed to appoint him because his training seemed to be more as an engineer than in theology. Finally they did appoint him, finding that he declared an intention to go to India whether or not he was appointed.

Clough's parents held high principles but were not practicing Christians. The youth longed to become a great lawyer. After several years of work first as a helper then as a U.S. deputy surveyor in the wilds of Minnesota, he enrolled in Burlington College in Iowa, a Baptist instituion that had been recommended to him by a surveying associate. The influence of the college and the Christian life of a roommate led young Clough to conversion.

Following graduation Clough married and, with his wife, taught school for one session, after which he spent a year in colportage work in Iowa. Then came mission board appointment. He, Mrs. Clough, and their small child departed for India with Lyman Jewett, who left his family in the U.S.

Called to the Madigas

Jewett cherished a dream. He longed for a mission station to be established in Ongole, a town of about 6,000 people and just over seventy miles up the coast from Nellore. Twelve years before he had made a mission trip into the area. He, Mrs. Jewett, and three Christian women from Nellore walked before dawn on New Year's Day in 1864 to the top of a hill overlooking the town and knelt in prayer at sunrise asking that a missionary might come there to establish Christian work. The place came to be known as "Prayer Meeting Hill."

After more than a year of language study in Nellore, in September 1866, the Cloughs settled in Ongole, fulfilling Jewett's dream.

Clough and many other pioneer missionaries in India hoped to win caste people to Christianity first. They felt that if this were done, those who were lower on the social scale would follow, and strong churches could be established. Most of the first converts in Ongole were of the Sudra caste, the menial workers. A dozen or so men of the highest castes professed faith and indicated their interest in receiving baptism. They refused to have anything to do with Christianity, however, if outcasts were received. They referred to the despised Madiga leather workers, who were also responding to the gospel; some had already been baptized in a fairly nearby village.

Seeking an answer to his problem, Clough walked into his study and absent-mindedly picked up an English Bible from a stack he had for distribution to British soldiers. The Bible opened to 1 Corinthians chapter 1 and the missionary read:

. . . not many wise . . . not many mighty, not many noble, are called. But God hath chosen the foolish things of the world to confound the wise,

. . . the weak things . . . and base things, and things that are despised .
. . that no flesh should glory in his presence.

Clough later recalled: "The impression made upon me as I read those words was overwhelming. It seemed like a voice from heaven."

This conviction was strengthened when his wife went into an adjoining room and picked up another Bible that also opened to the same passage, which she read. "It seems to be God's plan to save these outcasts first," she said to her husband.

Clough then told his wife of his own experience. He later wrote:

God had spoken to us. From that moment our doubts were gone. We believed that these poor, degraded Madigas were sent to us. We had our orders to go to the most despised class in India and bring them to the Lord Jesus. We went ahead, thereafter, nothing doubting.

Steady growth continued in the area, with virtually all of the converts coming from the Madigas. Clough went on evangelistic tours throughout that part of India. Sometimes he was away from home two months at a time and lived in his tent. For years he traveled on a fine white horse, which became a familiar sight to the people. The missionary was fearless in protecting the rights of Madiga Christians when their masters tried to take advantage of them, and the British authorities trusted him.

The Unexpected Harvest

Late in 1876 converts in and around Ongole numbered 3,269. Soon after this, famine struck the land due to virtually no harvests after monsoon rains failed to come for two years. People died of starvation by the thousands. Madigas, the lowest on the human scale and customarily living from hand to mouth, suffered most.

The government helped somewhat to alleviate the suffering. It distributed direct aid extensively, but only a fraction of the population could be helped in this way. It activated public work projects to provide employment such as the digging of Buckingham Canal, mainly for irrigation and slightly inland along the eastern coast.

John Clough, whose surveyor-engineer credentials were readily acknowledged by the authorities, took a contract for digging three and one-half miles of the canal. This necessitated the employment of about 3,000 workers at a time. He set up his tent on the bank of the canal, ten miles from Ongole, to direct the operation.

During the stress of this period, Clough's hair turned white. Although still in his early forties, nationals began addressing him with the title of respect, *tahta* ("grandfather,")—usually reserved for venerable old men.

Laborers rotated all the time. Some laborers, after working a few days or weeks, took their wages and returned to the villages to provide the needs of their families, and others replaced them on the canal job. Clough attempted to hire all who came, and to those unable to work he gave food freely. Perhaps thousands were saved from starvation by these means.

The thirty national pastors of the mission were the overseers, and Christians comprised about half of the working force. Religion became the principal topic of conversation on the job. Non-Christians as well as believers delighted in the story of Jesus and his love for all sorts of men, even the poor and despised.

Many of the laborers began coming to the missionary, asking for baptism. Realizing that other people might think they were coming simply out of gratitude for the help being given, Clough decided that no new church members would be received until the emergency had passed. There were no baptisms for fifteen months.

When the famine finally ended with good harvests in 1878, the missionary emphasized that applications for baptism would again be received, although he did his best to discourage anything like a mass movement. He called a meeting of church leaders and told them to advise most converts not to come at this time. They came anyway, by the thousands. A camp was set up for them on the Gundlacumma River at a place called Velumpilly.

The candidates were individually examined by missionaries and pastors, and many passed the test. On a single day—July 3— 2,222 were baptized in the river by six national pastors, working two at a time between sunrise and sunset. Within three days 3,536 were received and baptized. (On a personal mission trip to India some years ago, I was inspired to stand at that spot, on the bank of the Gundlacumma River, recalling with a prayer of thanksgiving what had happened there in 1878.)

By the end of 1878 membership in the predominantly Madiga church, which later divided into several churches, was 12,804—the largest of the denomination anywhere in the world. All of this occurred on a field that the mission board had been on the point of closing as a failure three times at least.

Principles of Work

Missionary recruits, many of them enlisted personally by Clough while on furlough in the U.S., went to India in rather large numbers. Clough raised funds for the establishment of a college and a theological seminary on the Telegu field. A hospital was later opened in Ongole and named for him.

Mrs. Clough died while in the U.S. in 1893. In the following year Dr. Clough (he had been awarded an honorary degree) married Emma Rauschenbusch, sister of the noted social service advocate, Walter Rauschenbusch. She had previously been a worker in the Telegu mission. The Cloughs retired to the U.S. in 1905. Clough had suffered a disabling accident when he was thrown from his horse while overseeing workers during another famine three years earlier.

John Everett Clough believed the gospel was for the whole person. He considered relief work and raising the level of life for Madigas part of his service as a missionary. Clough declared:

> There are some things I could not do. One of these was to preach to a crowd of hungry people. If the people of a village came to hear me, and I knew by their looks as they sat before me, that they had not had a square meal for days of weeks, I found I could not talk to them about the love of Jesus for them. I sent them off with a few coins first and told them to eat and then come back and hear my message.

Reflecting later on his missionary life he said,

> I have been asked what I would do if I were once more at the beginning of my missionary career. . . . I am glad I did all in my power to give educational opportunities to the people. I would again raise up a large native agency. I would again organize groups of believers, serving God

in simple ways of their village life. I would again do all I could for their social betterment. Above all, I would preach Jesus, the Christ, to them, and I would consider everything else subservient to that.

Membership of churches growing directly or indirectly out of Clough's work or that of his associates totaled 60,000 at the time of his death in 1910. Many people predicted that the results of such a mass movement as he experienced would not be lasting but they were. The Telegu work, especially among the Madigas, continued as a stronghold of Christian churches.

Note on Sources

Some of the statistics in this sketch come from "Mission to the Telegus" in the *Annual Reports* of the American Baptist Missionary Union. Quotations are from the books by Clough and Downie.

Selected Bibliography

Clough, John Everett. Recorded by Emma Rauschenbusch. *Social Christianity in the Orient: the Story of a Man, a Mission, and a Movement.* New York, 1914.
Clough, John Everett. *From Darkness to Light: Story of the Telegu Awakening.* Philadelphia, 1882 .
Downie, David. *The Lone Star: The History of the Telegu Mission of the American Baptist Foreign Mission Society.* Philadelphia, 1892.
Fishman, Alvin Texas. *For This Purpose: A Case Study of the Telegu Baptist Church in its Relation with the South India Mission of the American Baptist Foreign Mission Societies in India.* India, 1958.
Hines, Herbert Waldo. *Clough, Kingdom Builder in South India.* Philadelphia: Judson Press, 1929.